Twayne's United States Authors Series

Sylvia E. Bowman, *Editor*

INDIANA UNIVERSITY

Thomas Bailey Aldrich

THOMAS BAILEY ALDRICH

by **CHARLES E. SAMUELS**
Utica College of Syracuse University

 94

Twayne Publishers, Inc.   ::   New York

For
SHIRLEY

Preface

DURING the greater part of his literary career, Thomas Bailey Aldrich was esteemed as a minor novelist, a professional editor, and an important poet. He was, in fact, considered the equal of William Dean Howells and Samuel Clemens as a man of letters; and he was ranked favorably, especially as a poet, with his more famous predecessors, Longfellow, Lowell, and Whittier. His death, in 1907, produced the usual number of flattering obituaries and then he was forgotten—almost completely. Is it possible that Howells, the most discerning critic of his time, could have been so entirely wrong? In attempting to answer this question, this study has made no effort to resurrect Aldrich as a major American writer. His limitations were many and obvious. However, his contemporaries were not unjustified in their praise of his wit, his amusing short fiction, and above all, his poetic craftsmanship.

His short stories and his short novel, *The Story of a Bad Boy*, can deliver nearly a smile or chuckle for each page and are filled with an indulgent treatment of New England eccentricities and light-hearted local color. Aldrich's short fiction also has many delightful descriptions of the New England landscape, the sea, and a warm, nostalgic portrait of a decaying seaport town and its inhabitants. But Aldrich was not a Realist in the modern sense of the word; he concentrated on the pleasant aspects of life to the neglect of the sordid. However, he did not falsify in any other way, and his nostalgia was made palatable by his constant good humor. *The Story of a Bad Boy* has rightfully earned a place in literary history as one of the first attempts to portray realistically a young boy and boyhood.

But Aldrich's contemporaries regarded him primarily as a poet and their critical judgment was good. Aldrich deserves to be remembered as a skillful writer of light verse and as the author of a small body of excellent lyric poetry which, at the very least, makes him one of the best minor poets of his day. He was greater than the genteel school of Bayard Taylor and E. C. Stedman, with whom he is so frequently associated, and even today he can be favorably compared with the revered Lowell, Longfellow, and Whittier.

The author wishes to thank Mrs. Dorothy Sickels for her most generous editorial assistance; Mrs. Shirley Samuels, his wife, for her critical suggestions and her tireless work with the manuscript; and Utica College for providing the author much needed time to complete this study.

CHARLES E. SAMUELS

Utica College of Syracuse University
Utica, New York

Contents

Chronology

1836   Thomas Bailey Aldrich born in Portsmouth, New Hampshire, on November 11.

1841   The Aldrich family moves to New York City.

1846   The Aldrich family moves to New Orleans.

1849   Thomas Bailey Aldrich returns to his grandfather's home in Portsmouth to prepare for entrance to Harvard College. His father, Elias, dies in Memphis.

1852   Aldrich and his mother move to New York City to live with his uncle, Charles Frost, a successful merchant. Aldrich works in his uncle's countinghouse and writes poetry in his spare time.

1855   At nineteen, he publishes his first volume of verse, *The Bells: A Collection of Chimes,* and leaves the world of business. He becomes junior literary critic of the magazine *Evening Mirror* and then sub-editor of *Home Journal.*

1855- Works as editor and free-lance writer in New York
1864   City.

1865   *The Poems of Thomas Bailey Aldrich* published by Ticknor and Fields, the leading publishing house in America. Married to Miss Lilian Woodman on November 28th.

1866   Editor of *Every Saturday,* a periodical published in Boston.

1868   Twin sons born on September 17th.

1869   *The Story of a Bad Boy* published in book form, after having been serialized in *Our Young Folks,* a juvenile magazine.

1873   *Marjorie Daw and Other People* published.

1881- Serves as editor of *The Atlantic Monthly.*
1890

1890- Aldrich retires; travels to Europe several times; pub-
1900 lishes travel literature, sketches, poems, prose.

1896   Collected works appear in eight volumes.

1904   Son, Charles, dies of tuberculosis at 36.

1907   Dies on March 19th.

Thomas Bailey Aldrich

CHAPTER *1*

Boston-plated Bohemian

DURING THE LAST HALF of the nineteenth century, Thomas Bailey Aldrich was esteemed and respected as a major literary figure whose present and future claim to fame was unquestioned. Although he never claimed to be profound, he was a skilled artist whose amusing short stories and lighthearted novels were enjoyed by nineteenth-century readers who did not necessarily demand harsh realism and a tragic view of life. Moreover, Aldrich seldom attempted to reform his readers nor did he attempt to reform his age. His aim was to give pleasure by pointing out unnoticed beauty, by telling a good story, and by expressing warm human sentiments in highly polished verses which were sometimes sentimental, as he admitted, but which were often saved from bathos by the excellence of his light touch.

For Aldrich, dullness was original sin. He once claimed that Horace Scudder, who had succeeded him as editor of the *Atlantic Monthly*, was a greater man than Moses because, while Moses dried up the Red Sea once, Scudder dried up the *Atlantic* monthly. Aldrich's contemporary fame as a wit was unequaled. Mark Twain wrote of him: "Aldrich was always brilliant, he couldn't help it; he is a fire-opal set round with rose diamonds; when he is not speaking, you know that his dainty fancies are twinkling and glimmering around in him; when he speaks, the diamonds flash."[1]

The story of how a writer who earned Mark Twain's sincere admiration and the devotion of a small but discriminating audience could be forgotten so soon and so completely is in part the history of changing literary taste. Contemporary twentieth-century critics have dismissed Aldrich as merely one of the more competent writers of the declining New England literary tradition, the New England Indian summer. But modern readers have forgotten how delightful Indian summer can be at its best with its clear warmth and bright atmosphere. And, if they would read Aldrich, they would discover that he, too, has all of the Indian summer delights. His clear poetry and prose, his warm but amusing short stories, his bright wit, and his occasional nostalgic quality can still be enjoyed—if we take his work for what it is.

I *Bostonian Conservative*

In our time, the liberal writer has been welcomed; but, in our time, Aldrich could be typed only as a conservative. More specifically, he was a Boston conservative. As he was fond of saying, he was not of Boston but he was Boston-plated. He had arrived there in 1866, having left New York, the city where he had learned his trade, to return to New England, the home of his adolescent years. He assumed the position as editor of the eclectic weekly, *Every Saturday,* published by Ticknor and Fields, soon to become Fields, Osgood and Company. Aldrich's was indeed a journalistic position to be coveted. Within a few weeks, another young writer, William Dean Howells, also arrived in Boston; Howells became assistant editor of the esteemed *Atlantic Monthly.* Years later, Howells recalled that as editors under Osgood and Fields, he and Aldrich had about the same status. Undoubtedly association with the *Atlantic* carried greater prestige than *Every Saturday;* but, with his characteristic modesty, Howells admitted that Aldrich was "supreme in his place" while he was only "subordinate" in his.[2]

The young editors, who were alike in many ways, soon became friends. Both were young, self-educated, aspiring poets who had, by some miracle, been accepted by the aging, aristocratic, New England literary élite. While Aldrich had not as yet even semi-officially received the "laying on of hands" as Howells had, he had been published in the handsome Ticknor and Fields "Blue and Gold Series" which amounted to nearly the same. And Aldrich's fame as a poet was probably greater than Howells' who was amazed to find Aldrich so young. Howells, who had read Aldrich's poetry, had automatically assigned him to the generation of Holmes and Lowell.[3]

But though Aldrich and Howells had much in common and continued their bright, happy friendship to the end of life, there was something in Howells that made him finally leave Boston for New York and become more and more liberal in his thinking. Aldrich, who had just escaped from the exciting but hand-to-mouth life of New York's literary Bohemia, became more entrenched in Boston and consequently more conservative in his outlook.

The first few years of Aldrich's life in Boston largely explain his addiction to the American Athens. They were the happiest years of his singularly happy, untroubled life. He and his attractive, socially astute bride, the former Miss Lilian Woodman of New York City, naturally gravitated to Beacon Hill, first to a boardinghouse on Hancock Street and then to the little house on Pinckney Street decorated with "white muslin and pink ribbons, white muslin and blue ribbons." Mrs. Hawthorne named the house "Mrs. Aldrich's workbox," and Howells, to the couple's discomfort, always spoke of Aldrich's study as "Aldrich's boudoir."[4]

But the pink and blue ribbons were the only discordant note in an otherwise harmonious domestic happiness and in a varied cultural and social life. His publisher James Fields, and his brilliant wife Annie, invited the Aldrichs to the famous drawing room in their home at Charles Street; here they met

Longfellow, Lowell, Holmes, and Emerson. If the Aldrichs were impressed by the aging grandeur of the old guard, it is also true that at least Longfellow and Lowell welcomed the genial wit of Aldrich and that Mrs. Aldrich's social poise was equal to all these stately occasions. Later Longfellow called on the Aldrichs; and, because Aldrich had always revered Longfellow (actually attributing to him the first awakening of his own poetic inspiration),[5] this brief visit became one of his most treasured memories, not even surpassed by the visit of Charles Dickens, whom Mrs. Aldrich discovered in the "boudoir" seated in the easiest chair by the bay window.[6]

And there were also parties, formal dinners, afternoon teas, the theater, the opera, and the brilliant conversation of the Boston literati. Years later Howells, in a nostalgic mood, wrote to Aldrich from New York: "He [Clemens] is the only tie that binds me, here, to the old times (they *were* good, weren't they?) and I'm sorry he's got a time-table lengths away. . . . Here they are not so interesting as they used to be. Perhaps you and I were spoiled by the sort we used to meet in the eighteen seventies. You alone were enough to spoil one."[7] And less than one month later Howells again wrote to Aldrich in the same mood: "Those were the gay years, and bless God, we knew they were at the time."[8] Little wonder that Aldrich came to love Boston.

Also, aside from the gay years of Boston social life, Aldrich was pleased not only by the intellectual atmosphere of the city but by the inherent democracy of Boston society. The Brahmin class was, Aldrich discovered, an aristocracy of talent, in direct contrast to New York society which was not literary, but instead based its hierarchy primarily on birth and on money, as Aldrich knew from sad experience. Rejoicing in his welcome change of situation, he wrote to Bayard Taylor:

> You speak of the great city [New York] drawing us atoms into its literary vortex. I'm a-Tom that doesn't want to come

back just at present. I miss my dear friends in New York—
but that is all. There is a finer intellectual atmosphere here
than in our city. It is true, a poor literary man could not earn
his salt, or more than that, out of pure literary labor in
Boston: but then he couldn't do it in New York, unless he
turned *journalist*. The people of Boston are full blooded
readers, appreciative, trained. The humblest man of letters
has a position here which he doesn't have in New York. To
be known as an able writer is to have the choicest society
open to you. Just as an officer in the Navy (providing he is a
gentleman) is the social equal of anybody—so a knight of the
quill here is supposed necessarily to be a gentleman. In New
York—he is a Bohemian! Outside of his personal friends he
has no standing. . . . The luckiest day of my professional life
was when I came to Boston to stay. My studies and my
associations are fitting me for higher ends than I ever before
cared to struggle for. . . .[9]

But the literary friends and "associations" were not the
men they had once been. While the effects of post-Civil War
disillusionment were not so apparent in the late 1860's as they
were soon to become, they were there to the discerning eye.
The table of contents of Thomas Wentworth Higginson's
Cheerful Yesterdays[10] is symptomatic of the change. Following the chapter dealing with the Civil War are two chapters,
"Literary London Twenty Years Ago" and "Literary Paris
Twenty Years Ago." Interest in things European grew as
interest in the contemporary American scene dwindled.
Howells, a more objective observer of Boston, noticed that,
after the great issues of the war years had been solved, it was
difficult to show much enthusiasm about Civil Service reform.
It is significant that Bromfield Corey, when we first discover
him in *The Rise of Silas Lapham*, had been reading *Revue
Des Deux Mondes*.

Aldrich's magazine, *Every Saturday*, composed almost entirely of material pirated from English and French periodicals
of the day, helped supply readers with their demands for
things foreign. Aldrich, too, shared this interest, reading

"hundreds and hundreds" of French and English novels during his lifetime.[11] He joined the trek abroad, spending many summers in Europe collecting exotic bric-a-brac, visiting literary shrines, musing over the graves of Milton and Keats, looking for the odd, the atmospheric, the picturesque. Unlike his close friend and untiring world traveler, Bayard Taylor, Aldrich showed little interest in travel in the United States. Even the enormous problems of Reconstruction interested him not at all. Brought up to admire pre-war Boston, he was not disappointed with post-war Boston; and, if he realized that the old guard was becoming merely genteel, he was still willing to follow its members on their route to the past, to Europe, to literature rather than to the more demanding life of the Gilded Age.

II *The Not Such a Very Bad Boy*

If Boston confirmed Aldrich's tendency toward gentility and conservatism, his boyhood home, Portsmouth, New Hampshire, where he was born on November 11, 1836, had nurtured it. Soon after he was born, the family traveled extensively on business, finally settling in New York in 1841 for four years. Mr. Elias Aldrich's restless enterprise finally took him to New Orleans where he invested his money so securely in the banking business that he was never able to get more than half of it out again.[12] Young Thomas was ten years old when he left New York for New Orleans, his home for the next three years. His attachment for New England, "his native land," however, had already been formed in spite of the wanderings of the Aldrich family; and this move inspired the following poetic effort:

> Farewell to my birth-place, my fireside too!
>   A home in the South I am to get
> Though 'tis hard to tear myself from you
>   Still my native land I cannot forget.

Farewell to the woods where my voice echoed thru!
 Also to the river and fast running stream
Once more farewell to you!
 All now is past as a dream.[13]

While it is true that Tom Bailey, the "bad boy" of *The Story of a Bad Boy,* is in all essentials Thomas Bailey Aldrich, the novel is not literal autobiography. It is hard to believe, for example, that he was as ignorant of the North as was the fictional Tom Bailey who, when he heard he was going to be sent North to complete his education, expected that his grandfather "wore a blanket embroidered with beads, and ornamented his leggings with the scalps of his enemies." Aldrich had spent long summers in Portsmouth during the four years he had lived in New York; and, unlike Tom Bailey, he had already learned to love the rivers, the streams, and the forests of New England. It is true that certain vivid impressions of flamboyant New Orleans remained with him, "the weird-flaring torches of the negroes" who lighted the landings of the Mississippi boats, "the strange tropical beauty" of New Orleans, "the sweet blond saints in the New Orleans Cathedral";[14] but New England and especially Portsmouth did more to shape the boy than either New York or New Orleans.

In 1849, after three years in New Orleans, Aldrich was sent to Portsmouth to complete his education. His father returned to New Orleans in a futile attempt to repair his failing fortunes, but his restless, luckless life came to an end when he died of cholera on a Mississippi River steamer at Memphis in October, 1849. This loss meant much to Aldrich, more than he realized at the time; but years later, in *The Story of a Bad Boy,* he recalled its impact: "As the days went by my first grief subsided, and in its place grew up a want which I have experienced at every step in life from boyhood to manhood. Often, even now, after all these years when I see a lad of twelve or fourteen walking by his father's side, and glancing merrily up at his face, I turn and look after them, and am conscious that I have missed companionship most sweet and sacred."[15]

It is tempting but fruitless to wonder what Aldrich would have become had he had the influence of his enterprising, roving father during the formative years of his life. As it was, he concluded his education at Portsmouth under the staid, kindly direction of Thomas Darling Bailey, his grandfather, who is Grandfather Nutter of *The Story of a Bad Boy*. Grandfather Bailey, with whom Aldrich lived for the next three years, must have been dismayed at the daring enterprises of his son-in-law Elias, for Grandfather Bailey was far more conservative. Of the respectable middle class in the best New England tradition, he was regular in his habits, strict in his religion, and always kept the Sabbath with appropriate New England funereal gloom. He was undismayed by religious controversy of any kind. Toward the close of his life, Aldrich still remembered Grandfather Bailey's religious conservatism and envied "his unquestioning faith. He used to read a big Bible covered with rough green baize, and believe every word he read, even the typographical errors."[16]

A strict disciplinarian, he had ironclad rules about boating on the river and reading on Sunday; that is, reading anything but Baxter's *Saints' Everlasting Rest* or the Bible, but he was not severe and was never unjust. Aldrich learned to love and admire his grandfather; and, although Aldrich in later life did not share his religious convictions, he never lost his respect for the New England tradition of middle-class respectability so well exemplified by Grandfather Bailey.

Nor was the intellectual climate, at least as Aldrich remembered it, one designed to breed a revolutionary spirit. Portsmouth's revolutionary days were over. Once it had been a busy seaport, rivaling New York and Boston in importance; but its East India trade had stopped, despite its excellent harbor, and commerce passed Portsmouth by. Aldrich recalled it affectionately as a town "rich in grave yards with an indescribable atmosphere of respectability and comfort."[17] The busy, noisy wharves of the old days, where once was heard "the cries of stevedores and the shouts of sailors at the windlass," were silent in Aldrich's youth. The now "worm-eaten wharves, some of them covered by a sparse, unhealthy beard of grass, and the weather-stained, unoccupied warehouses" were still there but were crumbling with decay. No fortunes were being made or lost in Portsmouth, but the "several large cotton factories and one or two corpulent breweries" kept it prosperous in a moderate way. "It is a wealthy old town," Aldrich wrote, "with a liking for first mortgage bonds; but its warmest lover will not claim for it the distinction of being a great mercantile center."[18] The prevailing atmosphere of Portsmouth, as Aldrich knew it as a boy when it did so much to fashion his attitudes, was prosperous, respectable, middle class, and conservative in the New England tradition.

But Portsmouth was a good place for a boy to grow up. First, there was Grandfather Bailey's house, a low-studded, elm-shaded structure, at that time standing a little back from the main street. In the rear was a garden, the stables, and the carriage-house. The house itself was spacious and comfortably, though not luxuriantly, furnished. And for young Aldrich, who had led a nomadic life and never had a room of his own, the little hall bedroom his grandfather prepared for him gave him more satisfaction than anything else. In *The Story of a Bad Boy* he recalls his room in detail:

> Pretty chintz curtains hung at the window and a patch quilt of more colors than were in Joseph's coat covered the little truckle-bed. The pattern of the wall paper left nothing to be desired in that line. On a gray background were small bunches of leaves, unlike any that ever grew in this world; and on every other branch perched a yellow-bird, pitted with crimson spots, as if it had just recovered from a severe attack of the small-pox. That no such bird ever existed did not detract from my admiration of each one.

And he counted them—two hundred and sixty-eight birds, "not counting those split in two where the paper was badly joined." A washstand, a chest of drawers, a mirror, and a high-backed chair completed the furnishings. Not to be forgotten was the single-barreled shotgun, minus the trigger, placed on the wall at the foot of the bed by his grandfather "who knew what a boy loved, if ever a grandfather did."[19]

Unquestionably, next in importance to the hall bedroom was the attic. In those days, when large houses and large families were much more common, nothing was ever thrown away; it was just put in the attic. All who have explored the attics of old houses can understand Aldrich's delight in that part of the house, that "museum of curiosities" where met together "as if by some preconcerted arrangement, all the broken down chairs of the household, all the spavined tables, all the seedy hats, all the intoxicated-looking boots, all the split walking sticks . . ." and "the pots, the pans, the trunks, the bottles."

But of most importance was "the lidless trunk" in which he found "a motley collection of novels and romances, embracing the adventures of a Baron Trenck, Jack Shepard, Don Quixote, Gil Blas and Charlotte Temple. . . ."[20] Most of Grandfather Bailey's books were on religious subjects, but he did not insist that his young charge read them. Young Bailey, as Aldrich was known at the time, was free to spend hours in his room and in the attic reading and "believing every word he read, and no more doubting the reality of Sinbad the Sailor or the Knight of the Sorrowful Countenance than he did the existence of his own grandfather." By reading, he was able to escape to an "enchanted realm" where there were no lessons to get,[21] and no boys to smash his kite. This habit of extensive, if somewhat uncritical, reading developed during those leisurely, happy Portsmouth years stayed with Aldrich the rest of his life. It is natural that a boy of thirteen or fourteen would read for escape; but, as Aldrich grew older, his tastes did not change. True, he studied history at his leisure, but his reading of prose fiction was mostly the "hundreds and hundreds" of French and English novels he read during his lifetime.[22] As a boy, he turned to novels and romances for escape and pleasure; when an adult, he wrote novels and short stories to give others the same; he rarely dealt with social, psychological, or ideological problems in his fiction.

Soon after young Bailey arrived in Portsmouth, he was sent to school under the direction of the capable schoolmaster, Samuel De Merritt. Aside from the usual pranks perpetrated on him without malice by his classmates merely because he was a new boy and except for one epic fight with the school bully, young Bailey's school experience was a happy one. His easy assurance, ready wit, and happy spirit made him popular with his classmates and his teacher. Years later his old teacher wrote of him: "With the hundreds of pupils who have been under my instruction there is *not one* for whom I entertain a higher regard and a purer affection than Thomas Bailey Aldrich."[23] And Aldrich returned the high regard and respect in his portrait of Mr. Grimshaw, undoubtedly Samuel De Merritt, in his *The Story of a Bad Boy*: "I might make this part of my story more entertaining," he wrote, "by picturing Mr. Grimshaw [Samuel De Merritt] as a tyrant with a red nose and a large stick; but unfortunately for the purposes of sensational narrative, Mr. Grimshaw was a quiet, kind-hearted gentleman, though a rigid disciplinarian. He had a keen sense of justice, was a good reader of character, and the boys respected him."[24]

Young Bailey, the bad boy, really was not such a very bad boy; he was a diligent student, one who never played hookey and who learned his lessons well. Although he was not able to go on to Harvard as he had planned, he got a good basic education under Samuel De Merritt. He especially valued his training in grammar which made him, finally, the polished writer, the "purist" editor of the *Atlantic Monthly*. Later, after he had become famous as a writer and editor, Annie

Fields observed that he was "a worshipper of the English language and a good student of Murray's grammar."[25] He considered his training in grammar the most valuable part of his education.

But if Portsmouth did train him in the fundamentals of grammar and stimulate his interest in undiscriminating reading, it did little to stimulate his intellect. It did, however, provide him with vivid memories of a charming old town, temporarily by-passed by nineteenth-century commerce and trade—the perfect subject for the warm, nostalgic treatment of the local colorist. Portsmouth, its people, and its environs furnish the background for the greater part of Aldrich's fiction; and the sea, the river, and the surrounding forests were often vividly recalled in his poetry.

The old decaying wharves along the broad Piscataqua, especially the one at the foot of Court Street near his home, were an irresistible attraction to young Bailey, as they would be to any boy, especially one with a vivid imagination and a tendency to dream. "What a slumberous delightful lazy place it is!" he wrote. "The sunshine seems to lie a foot deep on the planks of the dusty wharf, which yields up to the warmth a vague perfume of the cargoes of rum, molasses, and spice that used to be piled upon it." He fancied that a man could sit "on the end of that old wharf very contentedly for two or three years, provided it could always be June."[26]

What boy could stay away from the broad, winding Piscataqua River with its many islands, perfect for explorations and beach picnics? And the leisurely flowing river, like the dusty wharves, inspired happy indolence and reverie in young Aldrich:

> To let the wherry listless go,
> And, wrapt in dreamy joy,
> Dip, and surge idly to and fro
> Like the red harbor-buoy;

> To sit in happy indolence,
> To rest upon the oars,
> And breathe the heavy earthy scents
> That blow from summer shores;[27]

Dreaming was as pleasant to Aldrich as fishing and swimming were to the less imaginative. Not that Aldrich did not participate in the usual boyhood sports; sometimes, however, he enjoyed even more being by himself, indulging in his lifelong habit of imaginative reverie—in his room, on the wharves, on the seacoast, and on the Piscataqua. The theme of isolation so prevalent in Aldrich's fiction and poetry derives in part from his boyhood habits of withdrawal from the world of reality to that of dreams and imagination.

Although the view of the Atlantic Ocean from Portsmouth is blocked by the scattered islands of the Piscataqua and by the mouth of the bay, the sea still exerted its influence on at least the younger population of the town. The lure of the sea was irresistible to Tom Bailey, in *The Story of a Bad Boy,* who tried to run away to sea; and to Grandfather Nutter, as well, who "at the age of ten years . . . [had] fled from the multiplication table and run away to sea." In fact, Tom Bailey recalled: "There was but one of our family who did not run away to sea, and this one died at birth."[28]

The sea, too, with its vastness, its mystery, its savage storms, stimulates the imagination as few other aspects of nature can. Aldrich's lifelong intimacy with the sea continually colored his fancy: "There is something in the illimitable expanse of sky and water that dilates the imagination. The folk who live along the coast live on the edge of a perpetual mystery. Only a strip of yellow sand or gray rock separates them from the unknown; they hear strange voices in the winds at midnight, they are haunted by the specters of the mirage. Their minds quickly take the impress of uncanny things."[29]

The town, too, with its rich past and placid present kindled Aldrich's imagination. A visitor to Portsmouth during Aldrich's youth would have been impressed by the old eighteenth-century houses and by some of the odd characters who lived in them.[30] There was the Langdon House, built of solid, dignified construction; the home of Governor John Wentworth, ardent royalist, who built what Aldrich thought "one of the handsomest old dwellings in the town"; the Warner House, with its eighteen-inch-thick walls and its lightning rod, reputed to have been installed under the personal supervision of Benjamin Franklin; and the John Paul Jones House, built in 1758.

Most of these old houses, mentioned by Aldrich in *An Old Town by the Sea*, are still standing—but the interesting types who occupied them are gone. They disappeared, Aldrich observed, in a railroad accident when the very first train made its run from Boston to Portsmouth. Before the advent of the railroad, the trip to Boston by stagecoach occurred but rarely during the lifetime of even the more well-to-do; and most people were born and buried in Portsmouth without once having left it. In those days, Portsmouth was provincial; but it also was individual, having many unique characters with "built-in plans and specifications" of their own. There were retired sea captains and merchants, elderly ladies with family jewels, and scholarly recluses. Even more eccentric was "the uninspired Thoreau," Benjamin Lear, who left his comfortable farm to live winter and summer in a miserable shanty, and the town half-wit and delivery boy, Wilbird Penhallow, with his sky-blue wheelbarrow. The proprietor of the town's only variety store was odd, too, because he violently objected "to the telegraph, to the railroad, to steam in all its application." Aldrich, who knew most of these interesting human oddities in his boyhood, later regretted that there were no longer any "odd sticks" to be found in the old town by the sea. The Portsmouth man, he observed, "has ceased to be parochial; he is no longer distinct; he is simply the Average Man."

Aldrich's boyhood in Portsmouth came to an end in 1852 when he was sixteen years old, but not before he had learned to respect the values of middle-class New England respectability and tradition. And his intimate knowledge of the old town by the sea, reinforced every summer for many years of his later life, remained a vivid memory.

III *New York City*

Before Aldrich left Portsmouth to work in the counting room of his Uncle Frost's commission house, he had developed a strong interest in literature, especially in poetry. Ever since he had discovered the trunk of books in his grandfather's attic, he had been an avid reader of fiction but he did not discover poetry until he first read Longfellow's "The Footsteps of Angels" while he was mourning the death of a friend. Five years later he wrote to his friend William Winter that he had never before felt such a gush of emotion: "The poem spoke . . . with a human voice." From that time on he loved all of Longfellow and became a poet.[31]

Aldrich had planned to go to Harvard to study literature with Longfellow, but his family could not afford to send him. Instead he went to New York to work for his uncle, who assigned him the job of checking bills of lading. Aldrich performed his countinghouse tasks dutifully but without enthusiasm; he much preferred, in spite of his uncle's tacit disapproval, to spend his leisure hours in his hall bedroom in his uncle's house at 105 Clinton Street, reading, writing verses, and indulging in his habit of imaginative reverie.

New York City in the 1850's and 1860's was for the sixteen-year-old Aldrich a dramatic contrast to the sleepy, provincial New England town he had learned to love. Unlike Portsmouth, New York was suffering growing pains. Outstripping

Boston and Philadelphia as the commercial and banking center of the East, New York was already a metropolis showing the effects of too-rapid growth; but it did offer a varied cultural and social life. In sharp contrast to stable, leisurely Portsmouth, New York was new, raw, and raucous. In the commercial sections of the city, the horse cars, wagons, carriages, and pedestrians crowded the narrow, dirty streets. Refuse disposal was shockingly neglected. Telegraph wires were strung everywhere with no regard for appearance.

The wide gap between the very wealthy and the very poor, intensified during the Civil War years, was already apparent in the 1850's. The crowded streets, filled with immigrants of English, Irish, and German origin, provided a cosmopolitan atmosphere; but these people sharply increased the ranks of the very poor and their tenements were breeding places of vice and crime. The 1857 *Harper's Weekly* carried articles that condemned the many cellar restaurants and bars, with secret entrances that were merely fronts for bawdy houses; complained about the unbelievable, inefficient police force that was unable to cope with the vicious children who congregated in the streets, in the hotels, and on the docks; noted the increasing habit of opium eating in New York; and estimated the number of prostitutes at five thousand. Aldrich's tendency to conservatism, his distrust of foreigners, and his resistance to change were reinforced by the appalling contrast between Portsmouth and busy, noisy, violent New York.

It is understandable, then, why Aldrich spent many of his leisure hours musing in his room and retreating from the traffic, the crime, and the business of the city. These hours spent with musing and poetry, however, were not completely lost. He began sending his verses to the *Sunday Atlas* where they were printed with favorable comment by the editor, and he finally sold a poem to the editor of *Harper's* for fifteen dollars, much to the amazement of his business-like uncle who asked, "Why don't you send the damned fool one every day?"

In 1854, when Aldrich was a mere nineteen, he took his poems to the publisher, L. C. Derby, who turned them over to George Ripley, his literary assistant, who approved them for publication. While the poems caused no sensation when they appeared as *The Bells: A Collection of Chimes*, at least the book was not a financial loss.[32] Soon after, however, Aldrich published a poem, "The Ballad of Babie Bell," in the *Journal of Commerce* and became famous overnight. The poem, an immediate popular success, brought the young, blond, curly-haired poet to the attention of the whole country. N. P. Willis, poet, essayist, and editor of the *Home Journal*, printed it in his weekly magazine, and thus introduced Aldrich to the literary and artistic circles of New York City.

Aldrich's introduction to N. P. Willis was fortunate. Willis, who with General Morris published *The Evening Mirror* and the *Home Journal*, was not only a respected literary figure but also an experienced journalist. He knew what the populace wanted to read, and he gave it to them.[33] Even his motto—"We should do our utmost to encourage the beautiful, for the useful encourages itself"—was not entirely idealistic; it was just the kind of motto that would appeal to his lady readers, those to whom he addressed himself and his magazines in the "feminine fifties." Willis was also a good judge of man's abilities. At least, he recognized Aldrich's potential editorial talent (suprisingly enough since Aldrich was a very boyish nineteen at the time) and tried him out as junior literary critic for *The Evening Mirror*.

Encouraged by his recent literary success, Aldrich, with some reluctance because of family affection, announced his intention to give up a business career and (in the jargon of the times) to devote his life to the Muse. In spite of his uncle's objections, he abandoned his ledgers forever and devoted his energies and talents to his new vocation with great success. Before the year was out, he was appointed sub-editor of the *Home Journal*, a post once held by Edgar Allan Poe.

Willis, whose health was beginning to fail, was spending most
of his time at his country estate and sending weekly copy to
New York. The actual work of editing this successful paper
was left in the hands of nineteen-year-old Aldrich since
General Morris concerned himself only with the business
affairs.

If Willis had seen Aldrich before he hired him, he might
have been reluctant to give him so much responsibility. Soon
after Aldrich had established himself as a competent editor,
he was lounging in the office one day, occupying two chairs,
one with his feet, when "an impressive looking man came in
and said, 'I'm Mr. Willis.'" It took the young editor "scarcely
a second to get his feet down from that chair to greet with
proper politeness the greatest contributor to the magazine of
his day."[34]

Aldrich continued to edit the paper successfully until he
left it in 1859 to join Henry Clapp's brilliant but ill-fated
Saturday Press. Aldrich's years as sub-editor of the *Home
Journal* were profitable ones. He gained wide editorial experience under the guidance of one of the best journalists of
the day. In 1856 he wrote to his new friend William Winter:
"I had no idea of what work is . . . till I became 'sub.' I have
found that reading proof and writing articles on subjects 'at
sight' is no joke. The cry for more copy rings through my ears
in dreams, and hosts of little phantom printers' devils walk on
my body all night and prick me with sharp-pointed types.
Last evening I fell asleep in my arm chair and dreamed that
they were about to put me to press, as I used to crush flies
between the leaves of my speller in school boy days."[35]

But the busy days were well spent, for the *Home Journal*
was a fine school of practical journalism. It was first of all a
literary magazine, assessed by William Winter as a "con-
spicuous literary authority of the hour."[36] Willis, a brilliant
if not profound essayist, contributed weekly essays on timely
topics, which established the quality of the paper as a whole.

The *Home Journal* also published poetry and fiction, book reviews, and general comment about the New York cultural scene, the theater, the opera, concerts and art. The magazine was addressed to the wives and daughters of the wealthy, aspiring middle class and Aldrich learned how to keep circulation up by tried and true journalistic tricks. "It was our policy," he explained, "to chronicle the staid comings and goings of our heavy advertisers, and never by any chance to print anything that would give offense to anyone. We always had two columns of this kind of thing each week."[37] The *Home Journal* also featured other circulation builders. One department entitled "Interesting to the Ladies" had comment on latest fashions. Another, "Little or Nothings," printed riddles, anecdotes, jokes, paragraphs on polite conduct and the like. For the young men and women about town, the *Home Journal* offered "Two or Three Things to Suggest Conversation at the Tea Table." One wonders at how many fashionable New York tea tables could be heard scintillating conversation on the subject "vegetable diet of no use," a *Home Journal*-suggested topic. The paper also carried announcements of marriages, deaths, engagements, and trips abroad, and it had a personal column that mentioned would-be fashionable names—obviously good for circulation.

Aldrich's experience on the *Home Journal* also made him well acquainted with New York society, such as it was. He certainly took no pleasure in merely chronicling the goings and comings of the ambitious middle class, but it was this experience that gave him his understanding of the New York fashionable set; and what he learned of it, he did not like. In the first place, New York society in the 1850's and 1860's was not literary; it was made up largely of a few old families who had managed to preserve their fortunes, plus the new rich who were treated rather cavalierly by the old guard. George William Curtis in his indignant, somewhat heavy-handed satire, *The Potiphar Papers* (1853), did what Aldrich could probably have done better and certainly should have done.

The Potiphar Papers satirized the very group Aldrich knew and was forced to cater to as editor of one of the first society magazines. Curtis saw the wealthy middle class as ignorant, vain, vulgar, and ostentatious. Mr. Potiphar earns thirty thousand dollars a year, but he is dominated by his extravagant wife who makes him leave his comfortable home to build a new one in a more fashionable district. Mrs. Potiphar and her set spend the summers at Newport and Saratoga and their winters in a round of extravagant, tasteless parties in brightly lighted ballrooms where they drink, perspire, and dance all night. It was a society of idle women and industrious men, of pampered daughters whose minds were filled with gossip but knew nothing of art, literature, or music.[38]

Even if Curtis' satire was exaggerated, which it probably was not, it contained enough truth to explain why Aldrich, who never lost his New England tastes and attitudes, had little in common with New York City society. His short story "Mademoiselle Olympe Zabriski" shows that he knew well the life of the young, wealthy New York bachelor and that he understood clearly the rigid distinction between the merely wealthy and the old Hudson River aristocracy. In certain moods, however, he did enjoy the life of the city: the salt sea breeze at Coney Island; floating down the Narrows; drinking lager beer in Hoboken; eating and drinking ices and punches at Mallards; watching the promenade concert at the Academy of Music; and looking at the crowds in the streets and the beautiful window displays during the Christmas season, especially the window at Tiffany's, on fire with diamonds.[39] But these moods were temporary. There was enough truth in Curtis' satire to make Aldrich eager to leave New York for the more genteel Boston at the first opportunity.

Although he found New York society life uncongenial, he

did enter the literary life of the town. He became friendly with the young, idealistic poets of the R. H. Stoddard set and with the lively Bohemians. The tendency to sentimentalism of the one and the sharp wit of the other contended for the domination of Aldrich's Muse for most of his life. Fortunately, the sentimental rarely had the upper hand completely; it was restrained by a saving sense of humor and by objectivity.

The writers who gathered at the Stoddards' salon in their boardinghouse on Tenth Street were dedicated poetasters, devoted to the cultivation of the Muse and intoxicated by their own young genius. Richard Henry Stoddard and his brilliant, creative wife were known as Dick and Lizzie to the crowd of some major but mostly minor artistic celebrities who made their pilgrimage to what Bayard Taylor facetiously called the "Shrine of Genius."[40] But one doubts that Taylor was so facetious after all, for he wrote to Stoddard in an unquestionably serious mood:

> We must both cling the closer to that worship which is the conservation of our lives—the unselfish homage of that spirit of art and beauty which men call Poetry. Let us work our way, what ever the toil and sorrow, from the vestibule to the chancel, from chancel to shrine, from the lowest footstool of the temple to the high priests place beside the altar. The same incense that reaches us will sanctify and embalm our griefs, they will share in our canonization.[41]

Taylor's nauseous effusions set the tone for the group, and they were matched by George Boker, another devotee at the Shrine, who exclaimed in a letter to Stoddard: "What a wonderful, what a holy gift is this Poetry! How should it not be prized, how should it not be cultivated."[42]

Taylor and Stoddard were joined by E. C. Stedman and his wife; Bierstadt, the painter; Launt Thompson, the sculptor; Edwin Booth, the actor; Aldrich and later his fiancée Lilian Woodman; and by many others whose fame was even more short-lived. From the focal point of the "Shrine" on

Tenth Street, the circle expanded to theater parties as guests of Booth, to afternoon teas and to brilliant parties at Bierstadt's and Launt Thompson's studio where the fervent discussions of poetry and art continued.

Aldrich, then famous as the author of the sentimental "The Ballad of Babie Bell" moved easily in the perfumed atmosphere of the "Shrine." He was not annoyed by the feminine sentiments of his associates for he, too, in the spirit of the times, had had his moments of tender musing. "My brain is so heavy it *won't* think," he had written to William Winter, "but my heart thinks, instead, and if there was ever a letter written from the soul this is one. . . ."[43] Although he had written in *The Bells*

> Perdition catch those lachrymosic bards
> That moan forever about weary earth
> And sea! as if their dismal dactytes could
> Improve it much!

his own sentimental, melancholy strain was apparent in his *Nest of Sonnets* which was privately printed in 1856. But his naturally cheerful disposition never gave way completely to the then fashionable morbid brooding; and in the poem "At the Cafe," which he printed in *Vanity Fair* in 1859, he was able to treat even his own love affairs with a light touch.

"At the Cafe" begins with the line "We were all very merry at Pfaff's," the famous Pfaff's beer cellar, the haunt of Walt Whitman and Henry Clapp, the King of Bohemia. There Aldrich met a group of sturdier wits than the pilgrims to Stoddard's "Shrine." The young writers, artists, and actors who gathered almost nightly in Pfaff's Cellar imported the name Bohemian from France; and, taking their cue from the recently deceased Edgar Allan Poe, they carried on his fight with New England respectability and New York boorishness, becoming the first organized Bohemia in America.[44] Too young to become members of the staid Century Club, too lively for the respectable Stoddard salon, and too intelligent and sincere to cultivate the approval of the wealthy class, they were, like all Bohemians, a declassed group and proud of it. Although Aldrich never became a true Bohemian (his break with the Stoddards came some years later), he did frequent Pfaff's with his close friends Launt Thompson and Edwin Booth. The Bohemians quickly dried up Aldrich's lachrymosic muse—or drowned it in Rhine wine and beer.

At Pfaff's, Aldrich could not count on the tender criticism and easy acceptance he found at the Stoddards. William Winter, the drama critic, recalled that among the Bohemians "candor of judgment was the inveterate custom." They had no use for writing that was "trite, conventional, artificial, laboriously solemn or insincere, and they never spared each other from the barb of ridicule."[45] Aldrich felt Walt Whitman's barb one evening when "the company was numerous and the talk was about poetry; 'Yes, Tom,' said the inspired Whitman, 'I like your *tinkles*: I like them very well.' "[46] The "tinkles" no doubt referred to Aldrich's first volume of poetry, *The Bells*. The criticism, which assigned Aldrich to the carillon school of poetry of Edgar Allan Poe whom Emerson had dismissed as "the jingle man," was good for the young poet who needed frankness more than the tolerant praise of the Stoddards.

The atmosphere at Pfaff's was conducive to informality and carefree talk. The cellar was roughly finished with a "few chairs and tables, a counter, a row of shelves, a clock and some barrels. At the east end of it, beneath the sidewalk of Broadway, there was a sort of cave, in which was a long table and after Clapp had assumed the scepter as King of Bohemia, that cave and table were pre-empted by him and his votaries, at certain hours of the day and night, and no stranger ventured to intrude into the magic realm."[47] Henry Clapp, Nantucket born, lecturer, writer, disciple of Fourier, and unsuccessful publisher, had lived in France long enough to speak French fluently and to cultivate "Frenchified" manners. His figure was apparently frail and his visage haggard, but there was nothing frail about his thought. He was "brilliant and buoyant in mind, impatient of the commonplace; intolerant of smug, ponderous, empty, obstructive respectability; prone to sarcasm . . . reckless of public opinion, but an apostle of freedom of thought."[48]

In 1858, Clapp started the ill-fated *Saturday Press* with William Winter as sub-editor; and in 1859 Aldrich left the *Home Journal* to become associate editor of the new publication. Aldrich's job on the *Home Journal* had been to chronicle the petty social activities of New York society: but, during his brief career on the *Saturday Press,* his task was the opposite since the aim of this publication was to satirize respectability in America. Clapp's outspoken, witty criticism of the contemporary scene was rare in his time. No one was safe from his barbs. He called Horace Greeley a "self-made man who worshipped his Creator." And a prominent churchman was, according to Clapp, "waiting for a vacancy in the Trinity."[49] Aldrich's brilliant wit was sharpened in the atmosphere of Bohemia; and, although he remained but a short time on the *Saturday Press,* the experience with Clapp and the other Bohemians helped to check his tendency to artificial melancholy and sentimentality. And his apprenticeship on the *Press* and the *Home Journal* prepared him well for his later, more important, editorial duties in Boston.

But Aldrich, though he enjoyed the beer and the repartee, was at best a part-time Bohemian. He continued his friendship with the Stoddards for a time and never broke off with Bayard Taylor, Launt Thompson, and Edwin Booth. His natural New England conservatism and reticence were shocked by the more flamboyant behavior of some of the Bohemians such as the infamous Ada Clare who cut her hair short, smoked, quipped at Pfaff's, and introduced herself as Miss Ada Clare and son.

Even more important, Aldrich still revered the New England writers and could not tolerate Henry Clapp's ridicule of Boston. After two unsuccessful attempts to get an appointment in the armed services and after a brief tour of duty as a war correspondent, Aldrich turned more and more toward New England. He spent many leisurely vacations in Portsmouth and much time in Boston courting the ward of Wendell Phillips, who finally, with firm feminine logic, rejected him because of his almost total lack of enthusiasm for Abolition.

In his literary career, Aldrich had been encouraged by Lowell who accepted his poem "Pythagoras" and who welcomed him "heartily to the *Atlantic*." Although Aldrich had not as yet succeeded in persuading the Boston publisher, Fields, to issue a collection of his poems in the deluxe "Blue and Gold" series, Aldrich had published in 1863 a collected edition of his poems in New York which won a long letter of kindly criticism from Oliver Wendell Holmes and one of commendation from Nathaniel Hawthorne. In the same year he became engaged to Miss Lilian Woodman, whom he had met through his close friend Edwin Booth; and he began to make serious plans for a more settled life. He worked hard as managing editor of the *Illustrated News* for a time, but, more important, he continued his assault on the *Atlantic Monthly* with his poems and with continuing success. Thus encouraged, he told his friend William Winter of his distaste for Bohemia and Bohemian writers and of his plans to leave New York.[50]

His chance to leave came in 1865 when Osgood invited him to edit *Every Saturday*. Aldrich wrote hastily to Bayard Taylor that "the Gods have been unexpectedly good to me . . . that Lilian and I are to be married on Tuesday. . . . We go immediately to Boston where I am to begin my duties with Ticknor and Fields. I . . . expect to be very happy, tho I confess the seriousness of the step I am taking makes me awfully thoughtful just now."[51] Aldrich was so happy to leave New York—remarking that he was lucky to escape with his

English intact—that he did not realize how valuable his experience there had really been. In New York he had found a sympathetic audience in the Stoddard set; constructive criticism from the Bohemians; and, most important perhaps, had gained indispensable experience as an editor.

The rest of his happy life needs but brief mention. Although his editorial duties with *Every Saturday* from 1865 to 1874 and with the *Atlantic Monthly* from 1881 to 1890 kept him busy, he still had the leisure to enjoy the companionship of his Boston friends, becoming more and more conservative, more deeply Boston-plated. The inheritance of a considerable fortune from a close friend made him independently wealthy, and he and his wife were able to travel extensively in Europe and at least once around the world.

The one great sorrow of his life came in 1904 when his son Charles Aldrich died of tuberculosis. The loss was a severe one, for Aldrich had had little training in adversity. Although he managed to maintain his cheerful exterior, it was a façade for a broken man. In 1907, after a brief illness, he died, saying with characteristic calm, "In spite of all, I am going to sleep; put out the lights."

CHAPTER *2*

The Mask and the Raven

ALDRICH'S BOOKPLATE, designed by his son Talbot, illustrates the son's knowledge of his father. The plate shows a raven perched not on the pallid bust of Pallas but on a comic mask. It is aptly descriptive of Aldrich's poetry. The melancholy strain is there, sometimes degenerating to mere sentimentality but it is never morbid, as was much of the sentimental poetry of the late nineteenth century. The raven is balanced by the comic mask. The mask is significant in another sense: there is often a chill in Aldrich's verse that comes from his reticence and objectivity—as though he were in truth holding a mask between himself and his audience. He finally became a Classicist in the sense of his admired Herrick, polishing and repolishing his verses; and, while he did not employ the *carpe diem* theme in the strict sense of the word, he did feel the sadness of the passage of time which he was usually able to express with a light touch.

I The Bells

In Aldrich's early poetry are found those qualities in conflict that he was able to resolve and unite in his mature verse. His best poetry contains a good deal of sentiment, as it should. His early poetry, however, tends toward the sentimental. In his first published collection, *The Bells*, there are too many lines like the opening ones in the poem about Chatterton: "This eve my heart is floating upon tears / A fallen rose-leaf floating on a stream."[1] And taking a cue from Edgar Allan Poe, who claimed the death of a beautiful woman to be the very best subject for poetry, Aldrich tolled his bells for the deaths of several beautiful women and, better yet, beautiful little girls.

It should be remembered, however, that *The Bells* was printed during the decade that has been aptly called "the feminine fifties" because female sentiment was the vogue. Then even sturdy wits like Mark Twain and Artemus Ward could be moved by the beautiful death of Babie Bell, who "only crossed her little hands," "only looked more meek and fair," and died.[2] And also, Aldrich was only nineteen, and tearful sentiment is a luxury the young can afford. Looking back on his early verse, the mature Aldrich smiled at his youthful melancholy musings:

> When I was young and light of heart
> I made sad songs with easy art:
> Now I am sad, and no more young,
> My sorrow cannot find a tongue.
>
> Pray, Muses, since I may not sing
> Of death or any grievous thing,
> Teach me some joyous strain, that I
> May mock my youth's hypocrisy![3]

But Aldrich was too harsh on himself. His "youth's hypocrisy" was a temporary pose; even at nineteen he knew it, for in *The Bells* we also find:

> Now by my Gods! Sir, you should have a cap
> You may believe, Sir, what your critic tells,
> You long have merited "a cap and bells."[4]

His critic could have been N. P. Willis, or Fitz-James O'Brien or the caustic Henry Clapp but certainly not Walt Whitman; for, though Aldrich at nineteen could accept criticism from his friends, he never forgot Whitman's caustic "I like your tinkles. I like them very well."[5]

II *Society Verse*

Not all of Aldrich's early verse was sentimental by any means. He became an accomplished writer of *vers de société,* a form no longer so popular as it was in the mid-nineteenth century. Society verse is light, sophisticated, flip, daring. At its best, it is brief and apt; and it adopts a mildly cynical tone toward love, flirtation, marriage, parties, balls, and teas. In *The Bells* it is refreshing to find:

> Fannie wears an open dress—
> Ah! the charming chemisette!
> Half concealing, half revealing
> Something far more charming yet.

And in the *Knickerbocker* (April, 1859) he wrote of a Lothario whose mistress caught him kissing another. The Lothario responds to her rage in the following vein:

> I saw a sort of maiden, northern lights
> Shoot up your cheeks and tremble in your eyes.
> I like such things. I like to see the wind
> Drive frightened clouds across tempestuous skies:
> I like the sea, and, when it's easily had,
> A very pretty woman, very mad!

But he concludes:

> I like wild things, as I have said, but then
> I should not want to own them. Who would be
> Proprietor of earthquakes, or loose hurricanes,
> Or comets plunging in celestial seas?
> Or wed a maid that could if she should please,
> Give him a touch of one and all of these?

These verses were not included in Aldrich's later collections and he would have destroyed them had it been possible. However, the skill he developed as a writer of society verse during his New York apprenticeship was used later in some excellent light verses that were retained in his final collection.

Also in *The Bells* there is a romantic sense of isolation, of aloofness, of a kind of sentimental snobbishness: "Nor do I view thee as the passing throng; / The surface pleases them: they do not probe." And in another early poem, "The Metempsychosis," he wrote:

> I know my own creation was divine.
> I brood on all the shapes I must attain
> Before I reach the Perfect, which is God
> And dream my dream, and let the rabble go.[6]

Of course this is not Aldrich speaking, necessarily, of himself, but he did not blush to write such romantic nonsense and to include the poem in his final edition. This mood of Romantic isolation was in part genuine, and it was to become Classical reticence and objectivity in his mature work.

Even as a mature writer, Aldrich was not an innovator. He never appreciated Whitman, had no use for the fad of dialect verse, and despised realism in poetry. He had respect for what he considered to be the Romantic traditions of English poetry:

> Romance beside his unstrung lute
>   Lies stricken mute.
> The old time fire, the antique grace,
> You will not find them anywhere,
> Today we breathe a commonplace,
> Polemic, scientific air:
> We strip Illusion of her veil;
> We vivesect the nightingale
> To probe the secret of his note.
> The Muse in alien ways remote
>   Goes wandering.[7]

As a young writer, however, he was often merely imitative. He tried his hand at Tennysonian blank verse in *The Bells* and it came out pure prose. "The Three Conceits" is obviously in imitation of Tennyson's "The Epic":

> It happened on a summer day that Hall
> And Walter Everland, a young poet

> And Arthur Thornburn and my humble self
> Were in a church-yard

One immediately recalls Tennyson's lines, and notes even the similarity of names:

> At Francis Allen's on Christmas-eve
>
> . . . .
>
> The parson Holmes, the poet Everard Hall
> The host, and I sat round the wassail-bowl.

The Ballad of Babie Bell and Other Poems is filled with such obvious Tennysonians as "Singing so cheerily / Living so merrily," and "O weary, weary night, that brings no rest to me!" Aldrich's "Invocation to Sleep" is imitative of Keats both in subject and diction—"The starry Air," "easeful sleep," "with viewless hand!" To prove that Aldrich's early verse was imitative not only of Tennyson and Keats but of Longfellow, Bryant, Shelley, and Poe would be to belabor the obvious.

But even the apprentice Aldrich had skill with words; and, like the early Keats, he had difficulty bridling his Pegasus. After his collected works came out in 1863, he received a warm letter of criticism from Holmes who warned: "You must not feed too much on 'apricots and dewberries.' There is an exquisite sensuousness that shows through your words and rounds them into voluptuous swells of rhythm as 'invisible fingers of air' lift the diaphanous gauzes. Do not let it run away with you. You love the fragrance of certain words so well that you are in danger of making nosegays when you should write poems. . . . Your tendency to vanilla-flavored adjectives and patchouli-scented participles stifle your strength in cloying euphemisms."[8]

Holmes was right. In one short poem, "The Moorland," are "dreary waste," "drizzling rain," "yawning cave," "snaky lightning," "sobbing rain," "wailing phantoms," "blind despair," "shadowy lips," "pathless woods," "mournful thing," "weary sounds," "kindred soul," "lonesome night," "ghostly rain," and "dreary waste." And Aldrich was guilty of such "nosegays" as

> When we crush a pouting bloom
> Ten to one we kill a Fairy!
> Maybe that the light perfume
> In our nostrils, sweet and airy,
> Is the spirit of the Fairy
> Floating upward. O, be wary![9]

In fairness to Aldrich, it should be noted that the above trifle was eliminated from all future editions of his poetry.

III *The Polished Poet*

When in 1865 the publisher Fields finally offered to Aldrich what amounted to the official sanction of the New England literati by publishing his poetry in the famed "Blue and Gold" series of Ticknor and Fields, Aldrich's fame as a poet was established; his literary apprenticeship was finished. Not that he did not continue to develop. He was never satisfied with his work, for he eliminated and revised as long as he wrote. The definitive 1897 collection of his poetry "which include[s] all the lyrics and poems that the author desired associated with his name."[10] contains but a small fraction of his published poems. Of the 1863 edition by Rudd and Carleton, Aldrich saved only eighteen of fifty-one poems. Of the 1865 "Blue and Gold" collection, he saved twenty-eight of seventy poems for the definitive edition.

As Aldrich matured as a poet, his sentimentality was curbed. He did reprint "The Ballad of Babie Bell' in subsequent collections because it had been so widely printed without his consent and often incorrectly; but, on the whole, his sentimentality is tempered with restraint and economy. "Broken Music," a poem about a young girl who had published a book of poetry but had soon after committed suicide, is a far cry from his early poetry. In it the theme of the death

of a beautiful woman is handled with gentle dignity and
genuine emotion. It deserves quoting in part. After imagining
what she might have looked like, Aldrich continues:

> I know not; I conjecture. 'Twas a girl
>   That with her own most gentle desperate hand
> From out God's mystic setting plucked life's pearl—
>   'Tis hard to understand.
>
> So precious life is! Even to the old
>   The hours are as a miser's coins, and she—
> Within her hands lay youth's unminted gold
>   And all felicity.
>
> .   .   .   .
>
> This is her Book of Verses—wren-like notes,
>   Shy franknesses, blind gropings, haunting fears;
> At times across the chords abruptly floats
>   A mist of passionate tears.
>
> A fragile lyre too tensely keyed and strung,
>   A broken music, weirdly incomplete:
> Here a proud mind, self-baffled and self-stung,
>   Lies coiled in dark defeat.[11]

The appropriateness of the comparison in the last verse
needs little comment. While it is not particularly original, it
is skillfully developed. On first reading, it would seem that
Aldrich had changed his image from lyre to serpent. However,
when the string of a lyre snaps, it does coil and sting itself—
and sometimes the one who is playing it. One is made to feel
the tension that must have driven a sensitive young woman
to suicide. Aldrich had learned to adopt the appropriate tone,
one of meditative musing on the mysteries of the mind, tinged
with genuine compassion.

Although Aldrich continued to sing in a minor key on occasion, he lost his taste for melancholy verse. His mature mood
is best expressed in his own words:

> I'll not confer with sorrow
>   Till tomorrow;

But Joy shall have her way
This very day.

. . . .

Tears if you will—but after
Mirth and laughter,
Then, folded hands on breast
And endless rest.[12]

He expressed a similar mood even better in one of his quatrains:

I little read those poets who have made
A noble art a pessimistic trade,
And trained their Pegasus to draw a hearse
Through endless avenues of drooping verse.[13]

Aldrich also outgrew the sophisticated pose he had adopted in his *vers de société* and developed a truly sophisticated wit. His poem, "An Elective Course," subtitled "Lines Found Among the Papers of a Harvard Undergraduate," is a pure delight. While the intellectual world, including his beloved Tennyson, was dismayed by the new scientific theories and discoveries, especially evolution, Aldrich remained undisturbed. In "An Elective Course" he said, in effect, why worry about how we got here? Rather, enjoy what we have and always have had—beautiful women. The narrator in the poem compares his Hilda to all knowledge. He, the narrator, does not have "to go very far / To learn what heavenly bodies are." Evolution is important to him only because Hilda evolved; that is enough. He "leave[s] it to the addle-pated, to guess how pinks originated / As if it mattered."

But, of course, the charm of the poem is in its expression. Written in quite regular iambic tetrameter, it is given variety by the use of spilled-over lines as in "The loveliest book that ever man / Looked into since the world began / Is Woman!"[14] Although the meter remains constant, the lines vary in length from "Siberia and Italy" to "Frowns that gloom and smiles that glow." Moreover, the rhymes are unexpected and amusing: *Italy* with *geography, progressed* with *our rest, o'erhead* with *inhabited, conquered us* with *Copernicus, chasm* with *protoplasm, addle-pated* with *originated*.

This poem is more wiry than the dainty, perfumed *vers de société* of his New York period. It is, in fact, a Cavalier poem. "At a Reading" is another in the same mood. It begins

> The spare Professor, grave and bald
> Began his paper. It was called,
> I think "A brief Historic Glance
> At Russia, Germany, and France."
> A glance, but to my best belief
> 'Twas almost anything but brief—
> A wide survey, in which the earth
> Was seen before mankind had birth;
> Strange monsters basked then in the sun,
> Behemoth, armored glyptodon,
> And in the dawn's unpractised ray
> The transient dodo winged his way;
> Then by degrees, through silt and slough,
> We reached Berlin—I don't know how.[15]

The evening is saved by Hypatia whose elastic figure, "like a pond-lily taking air," charmed the bored listener. The situation is commonplace; there is no intellectual content; but it is a graceful tribute to a woman and a gentle "spoofing" of Boston intellectuals. But the real quality in the poem is again the deft prosody and the whimsical rhymes and diction.

Aldrich's subject matter is most often Romantic, but his treatment is frequently Classical in the Cavalier manner. He acknowledged his debt to Herrick in "Hesperides":

> If thy soul, Herrick, dwelt with me,
> This is what my songs would be:
> Hints of our sea-breezes blent
> With odors from the Orient;
>
> . . . .
>
> Wine-red jewels that seem to hold
> Fire, but only burn with cold;

Antique goblets, strangely wrought,
Filled with the wine of happy thought,

. . . .

Hopeful as the break of day;
Clear as crystal; new as May;
Musical as brooks that run
O'er yellow shallows in the sun;

. . . .

Brief as thy lyrics, Herrick, are,
And polished as the bosom of a star.[16]

Aldrich was like Herrick in more ways than one; and, had
he lived in the seventeenth century, he would have been one
of the "tribe of Ben." Like Herrick, he did not consider poetry
a fit vehicle for the expression of profound ideas nor did he
concern himself to any extent with the political or the social
scene. He did not attempt a *magnum opus*. He recognized his
limitations and wisely decided to work well within them.
Herrick might have written Aldrich's poem, "Lyrics and
Epics," of himself:

> I would be the Lyric
> Ever on the lip,
> Rather than the Epic
> Memory lets slip.
>
> I would be the diamond
> At my lady's ear,
> Rather than the June-rose
> Worn but once a year.

Herrick's love of flowers might have led him to reverse the
preference in the last four lines, but he would have approved
the sentiment.

Like Herrick's, Aldrich's verses also are "filled with the
wine of happy thought." In "The Two Masks" he wrote:

> I gave my heart its freedom to be gay
> Or grave at will, when life was in its May;
> So I have gone, a pilgrim through the years,
> With more of laughter in my scrip than tears.[17]

But like most Classicists from Horace to Housman, Aldrich could not escape the sad awareness of the passage of time and the mystery of death. Even the Anacreontic "Amontillado" ends on a pensive note:

> When pale Charon comes
>   To row me o'er his ferry,
> I'll fee him with a case
>   Of Amontillado sherry!
>
> What! the flagon's dry?
>   Hark old Time's confession—
> Both hands crossed at XII,
>   Owning his transgression!
>
> Pray, old monk, for all
>   Generous souls and merry;
> May they have their share
>   Of Amontillado sherry![18]

Although Aldrich was not morbid about the problem of death, as the seventeenth-century wits often were, he did ponder about some of its paradoxes, especially the odd fact that in the midst of seemingly perfect happiness comes the thought of death which, at that moment, is most sharply felt:

> I wonder what day of the week,
> I wonder what month of the year—
> Will it be midnight or morning,
> And who will bend over my bier? . . .
>
> —What a hideous fancy to come
> As I wait at the foot of the stairs,
> While she gives the last touch to her robe,
> Or sets the white rose in her hair.
>
> As the carriage rolls down the dark street
> The little wife laughs and makes cheer—
> But . . . I wonder what day of the week,
> I wonder what month of the year.[19]

A glance at the table of contents of Aldrich's collected works shows that the themes of death and the passing of time were not infrequent ones. In "The Poet" he tells us that the poets of the future will "baffled lie at Nature's feet / Searching the volumes of her mysteries, / And vainly question the fixed eyes of Death."[20] "The Undiscovered Country," "Sleep," "Even this Will Pass Away," "I Vex Me Not with Brooding on the Years" are excellent sonnets; nearly perfect in form, they express Aldrich's poetic musings on these universal subjects of death and transience. There are no profound solutions, but there is genuine emotion, neatly expressed.

In genteel Boston, Aldrich could not express his appreciation for beautiful women in the lusty manner of the seventeenth century. The Cavalier spirit was in him, however. His poetry and his prose are filled with lovely portraits of beautiful women. There are the "dancing girls of Astrakhan" who float in like mists from Fairy-land!

> And to the low voluptuous swoons
> Of music rise and fall the moons
> Of their full brown bosoms.[21]

And there is Nourmalee, who is described in sensuous detail from her narrow waist to the mole close to her lip but who turns out, unfortunately, to be like Marjorie Daw, a figment of the imagination. And Pepita—"scarcely sixteen years" old but nearly mature, with her red lips and with her coal black hair that are dulled a trifle by, of all things, the radiance of her eyes and teeth—is hauntingly beautiful. There are also the native New England girls—Fanny, Hypatia, Hilda—who are described with warm appreciation.

Aldrich never considered himself a regional poet nor a nature poet, but his poems do contain many descriptions of the New England scene, especially of the New England coast. It has been noted that Aldrich can be considered a forerunner of the Imagists.[22] It is true that in his passion for economy of expression, for finding the exact word, and for his concreteness, he resembles the Imagists, especially when he describes the native scene. He loved the sea, the forests, the rivers, and the gardens of Maine and New Hampshire; and he created poetic descriptions and scenes that should be lasting. Two poems, "Fireflies" and "Memory" in particular, are remarkable for their clarity and sharpness of outline:

> See where at intervals the firefly's spark
> Glimmers and melts into the fragrant dark;
> Gilds a leaf's edge one happy instant, then
> Leaves darkness all a mystery again.[23]

And "Memory" is also a miniature masterpiece for its compression and vividness:

> My mind lets go a thousand things
> Like dates of wars and deaths of kings,
> And yet recalls the very hour—
> 'Twas noon by yonder village tower,
> And on the last blue noon in May—
> The wind came briskly up this way,
> Crisping the brook beside the road;
> Then, pausing here, set down its load
> Of pine scents, and shook listlessly
> Two petals from that wild-rose tree.[24]

He also described the wild, New England winter coastline in the first two verses of "Landscape":

> Gaunt shadows stretch along the hill;
> Cold clouds drift slowly west;
> Soft flocks of vagrant snowflakes fill
> The redwing's frozen nest.

> By sunken reefs the hoarse sea roars;
> Above the shelving sands,
> Like skeletons the sycamores
> Uplift their wasted hands.[25]

In the ballad "Seadrift" he is able to express in a few brief lines the terror of a storm along the coast:

> The sea it moans over dead men's bones,
> The sea turns white in anger;

The curlews sweep through the resonant air
    With a warning cry of danger.

The star-fish clings to the sea-weed's rings
    In a vague dumb sense of peril;
And the spray, with its phantom fingers grasps
    At the mullein dry and sterile.[26]

But Aldrich rarely described nature for its own sake; it is
often the setting for a fanciful reverie. "On Lynn Terrace,"
for example, begins with a description of the seacoast and
its pleasures; but, as the poem progresses, it is concerned with
Aldrich's memories of the places he has visited: the Alhambra,
Calais, Venice, and many more. The poem closes with

For me the clouds; the ships for me;
    For me the petulant sea-gull takes its flight;
And mine the tender moonrise on the sea,
    And hollow caves of night.[27]

The same device is apparent in the sonnet "At Bay Ridge,
Long Island." In fact, many of Aldrich's poems begin with
descriptions of nature but not infrequently lead to more than
mere description. Though he did not believe with Emerson
that "natural facts are symbols of spiritual facts," he did use
nature for far more than a pretty pictorial device. The sonnet,
"Even this Will Pass Away," has a description of a May morning, but it is really a musing treatment of the theme of
transience. "Spring in New England" is only partially about
spring; it is actually a tribute to the Civil War dead.
"Reminiscence" begins with a description of the rigors of
New England winters, but it is a sonnet about the possibility
of pre-existence. "Books and Seasons" again begins with a
picture of a May morning, but it is really concerned with
loveliness that is "All too sweet"; thus "this springtime riot
must be tempered with a little sadness." Although Aldrich
was not primarily a Nature poet, his sharp and observant

descriptions of his environment make his poems more credible, no matter how fantastic or abstract the subjects may be.

Aldrich's more ambitious narrative and dramatic poems— "Wyndham Towers," "Judith and Holofernes," "Friar Jerome's Beautiful Book," and a few others—have been forgotten; and no attempt will be made to revive them in this study. Aldrich, like so many others, did not escape the dying vogue of the medieval tale, and he wrote in that vein skillfully but without distinction. Also, these works are too sentimental and moralistic for modern taste; and he did not add anything significant to the genre or its method of treatment.

This statement cannot be made of his treatment of the Oriental theme. The vogue for Oriental poetry has been so completely forgotten that it is hardly mentioned in the literary histories, probably because it flourished primarily among the minor poets who have fallen completely out of fashion. It had its roots, of course, in Byron and Tennyson; but it was the so-called "genteel poets" of the last half of the nineteenth century who carried on the tradition in America. And their audience shared their interest. Hamlin Garland complained that he could find no reference to Illinois or to Wisconsin in the magazines of the time (1885): "The Eastern readers of these magazines were not interested in the monotonous mid-West. They were eager for the plains of Araby and the Vale of Cashmire. . . ."[28] Not only the poets but the painters of the era took their cue from Delacroix, who had painted scenes from Byron's poems; and they turned out hundreds of slick canvases on such exotic subjects as "The Slave Market," "The Slave Girl," "The Odalisque," "Fatima," "The Harem," and others which were nothing more than excuses to paint voluptuous nudes. The whole trend came to its revolting climax in Hollywood with the mass hysterical vogue of Rudolph Valentino and his famous film, *The Sheik.*

Aldrich did not escape the passion for the Oriental, but he was not entirely uncritical of it. His second book of poetry,

The Course of True Love Never Did Run Smooth, was a tale of tragic love, set, of course, in mysterious Arabia. Although it won some critical notice at the time and a letter from Longfellow inviting him to visit the great poet in Boston, Aldrich realized it was a fledgling work and retained only a few short passages from it in subsequent collections of his poetry. But Aldrich did feel the appeal. In "Reminiscence" he speculates:

> . . . I must have known
> Life otherwhere in epochs long since fled;
> For in my veins some Orient blood is red,
> And through my thoughts are lotus blossoms blown.[29]

But this is only one mood. In "The Crescent and the Cross" he compares the two religions and admits that "Both stained with blood, and sacred made by faith, / By tears, and prayers, and martyrdom, and death." However, when he compares them, he concludes that "The waning Crescent lacks divinity: / It gives me dreams of battle, and the woes / Of women shut in dim seraglios."[30]

And in "The Sultana" he describes the luxurious furnishings of an Eastern palace and the beauty of the Sultana who can be seen in her "gilded chamber," but he recognizes that she is little more than a prisoner and concludes:

> But pallid, luminous, cold,
> Like a phantom she fills the place,
> Sick to the heart, in that cage of gold,
> With her sumptuous disgrace.[31]

Unlike his friend Bayard Taylor, who traveled extensively in the East and who had written much sensuous Oriental love poetry, Aldrich, like most of the Arabic bards, knew the Orient only second-hand. Had he lived among the Arabs or Turks as Taylor did, the urbane and urban Aldrich would have despised them. His knowledge of the East was, for the most part, from books; and it can be said, to his credit, that he did not accept all of the romantic nonsense that was written in the vein of "When the Sands of the Desert Grow Cold." He sensed that passionate, barbaric love in a setting of Eastern splendor was only a part of Oriental culture—and a small part at that. He had the sensitivity to feel the "woes of women shut in dim seraglios." He wrote his Oriental poetry in exactly the same way that Spenser or Milton wrote pastoral poetry: he accepted Orientalism as an established literary tradition. After all, he had Thomas Moore, Byron, Tennyson, and Fitzgerald as precedents; but Aldrich had also mistaken a fad for a genuine tradition.

Fortunately, he included only a very few Oriental poems in his definitive edition, but among them is one worth remembering. "When the Sultan Goes to Ispahan" is sportive Orientalism. In this poem, Aldrich, with tongue in cheek, revels in his love for exotic diction. "The flower of the harem, Rose-in-Bloom" orders a feast:

> Glittering squares of colored ice,
> Sweetened with syrop, tinctured with spice,
> Creams, and cordials, and sugared dates,
> Syrian apples, Othmanee quinces,
> Limes and citron, and apricots,
> And wines that are known to Eastern princes;

And she prepares the scene:

> Scattered over mosaic floors
> Are anemones, myrtles and violets,
> And a musical fountain throws its jets
> Of a hundred colors into the air.
> The dusk Sultana loosens her hair,
> And stains with the henna-plant the tips
> Of her painted nails, and bites her lips
> Till they bloom again;

But Rose-in-Bloom does not bud and bloom for the Sultan
Shah-Zaman. The Sultan has gone to the city of Ispahan,
while Rose-in-Bloom is at the palace

> . . . in this Eastern Paradise,
> Filled with the breath of sandal-wood,
> And Khoten musk, and aloes and myrrh,
> Sits Rose-in-Bloom on a silk divan,
> Sipping the wines of Astrakhan;
> And her Arab lover sits with her.

Aldrich, in the mood of his *vers de société,* concludes:

> Now, when I see an extra light,
> Flaming, flickering on the night
> From my neighbor's casement opposite,
> I know as well as I know to pray,
> I know as well as a tongue can say
> *That the innocent Sultan Shah-Zaman*
> *Has gone to the city of Ispahan.*[32]

By combining orientalism with *vers de société,* Aldrich
spoofed both. His common sense and his sense of humor
saved him from the excesses of the Oriental vogue.

Although Aldrich did not concern himself with the contemporary scene as a rule, he did so on occasion. He had little
sympathy for Abolition, but he was moved by the sorrow and
horror of the Civil War. His brief war experience as a correspondent produced one memorable poem, "Fredericksburg,"
in which he vividly describes the breathless moment when
the battle actually begins. The poem opens in a quiet mood:
the stillness of the early morning, the moonlight on the church-
yard, the waning stars and then—sudden conflagration, gun-
ners holding their breath, a signal rocket, and "the black
squadrons wheeling down to Death."[33]

His ode on the unveiling of the Shaw Memorial in 1897
is forced and hackneyed. He could not write occasional verse

with ease, and he wisely attempted it infrequently. In his "Spring in New England," however, he was able to blend a memorial tribute to the Civil War dead with excellent descriptions of the New England spring. It is not only one of Aldrich's better poems; it is one of the better poems inspired by the Civil War.

He also felt something of the pessimism of the period, a pessimism that was growing as both science and the higher biblical criticism continued their assault on traditional religion, an assault which tended to leave man friendless in a hostile or an indifferent universe. In the mood of Stephen Crane, who compared the world to a rudderless ship, Aldrich wrote "The Shipman's Tale," comparing the world to a wrecked ship "swept at last into the nameless void."[34] And he wrote an impassioned denunciation of the immigration laws in "Unguarded Gates." The less one says of it the better.

Aldrich realized that the moods of "The Shipman's Tale" and "Unguarded Gates" were not characteristic to him. His disposition was sunny; furthermore, he did not really believe the immigration laws a fit subject for poetry. He tried to express universal sentiments in perfectly wrought verse and, at his best, succeeded. He was a good critic of his own work, and the 1897 edition of his collected poetry that contained his final selection is uniformly competent. If some of his longer narrative poems and if some like "The Ballad of Babie Bell" that Aldrich felt compelled to print, although he realized their inferiority, were eliminated, a single volume of uniformly excellent verse would remain, a volume that would assure Aldrich a place as one of our best minor poets.

Aldrich did not attempt to embrace the universe in his work. Barbaric yawps were not for him. Like Herrick, his English counterpart, he was content to work skillfully in smaller compass. Aldrich was to Whitman as Herrick was to Milton. Epic poets, "realistic" poets, propagandistic poets, and philosophic poets all have their place. But we are inclined to forget that the pure lyricist has his place as well. England has not forgotten Herrick because she has a Milton, nor should the United States forget Aldrich because she has a Walt Whitman.

CHAPTER 3

Short Stories and Sketches

ALDRICH'S SHORT STORIES are pure delight. We may look to other writers for harsh realism, profound ideas, powerful emotion, and social consciousness. For the most part, Aldrich was not concerned with these qualities in his stories. At least two of them, "Marjorie Daw" and "A Struggle for Life," are still widely read, and they are well told with an art that conceals art. They are not tragic and melodramatic nor are they burdened with a message. They are not concerned with the then popular themes of seduction, romantic adventure, and horror; nor do they preach to us about social injustice, morality, and crime.

The short stories are about romantic love but not in a "swooning" sense. Love is treated with restraint and a quiet sense of humor. They are about odd domestic situations in perfectly believable settings in New York City, Boston, or Portsmouth. They are able to create suspense concerning ordinary events and to relieve it suddenly in surprise endings that are, however, prepared for skillfully. They have their limitations, of course. They are not allegoric or symbolic. They have but one level of meaning, if they can be said to have any meaning at all. They should not be compared with the stories of Hawthorne and Melville, but they are superb stories in their own right: sophisticated, witty, and amusing.

So often writers take themselves seriously. Some of them should; they have something to teach or they have an important mission. Others try to impress their readers with their perception, their singular sensitivity and subtlety. It is a pleasure, at times, to read an author like Aldrich who is content to be himself, who has no mission, literary or otherwise; who does not tease our intellect; and who is content to tell a story as well as he can. While Aldrich's stories may not be intellectually stimulating, they are never boring nor ponderous.

I *Early Short Stories*

Aldrich's early fiction, like his poetry, is not remarkable. Much of it is imitative, loosely constructed, and sentimental. The influences of Poe and Hawthorne are evident, and so is the sentimental side of Dickens. An early story, "What Jedd Pallfry Found in the Coffin," is interesting not only because it shows, when it is compared to his later work, how much Aldrich improved, but because it is also a good example of the run-of-the-mill literary fare that the readers of the "feminine fifties" found palatable. It is the story of a mean, old undertaker, Jedd Pallfry, who had turned his daughter and her illegitimate child from his door. The child, a boy, who was left to shift for himself, finds his way to the funeral parlor of Pallfry; and, since he was cold, starving, and exhausted, he climbed into a coffin and slept. Pallfry was out of the parlor at the time. When he returned and saw what was in the coffin, he "started, but not with fear. He felt something trembling, throbbing, warming his bosom. It was only his heart melting! The nature and humanity of the man had broken their fetters like reed, and the love which had lain in a trance for a dozen years, rose up within him, and would be heard! His heart knew the little stranger in the coffin and he bent over him with a tenderness that belongs to woman."[1]

Readers in those days did not find such ridiculous plots and artificial sentiment ludicrous. For modern readers, of course, the less said of Jedd Pallfry and his heart the better. In 1862, however, Aldrich published a collection of stories and sketches called *Out of His Head.* The title story is a series of loosely connected, lurid incidents; and the recounting of one situation is enough to give the tone of the whole. A young man falls in love with a girl who dies while he is "out of his head." Although she is dead, he thinks he sees her walking into the woods toward a pool. He follows just in time to see her transformed into a water lily.

Not all of the book is made up of such fanciful nonsense, however. One section of it, called "Peter Lynde's Sketch Book," contains some writing that shows promise of what Aldrich was to become. "Père Antoine's Date-Palm" is a sentimental tale of two friends in New Orleans, Antoine and Emile Jardin, who are studying for the priesthood. Both fall in love with an orphan girl from a nameless island in the Pacific, but Emile wins her. The lovers flee to the Pacific, and Antoine becomes a priest. Later, Père Antoine learns that his former friend and his wife had died and that their daughter is now being put in his care. She comes; he loves her tenderly but she dies longing for the palm trees of her native island. When she is buried in the garden, a date palm miraculously grows on her grave.

The plot is ordinary enough, and from even this brief summary the built-in sentimentality is apparent; but, somehow, it does not offend. Aldrich kept it in his 1897 collection and had it privately printed in 1866 and sent it to his friends. Mrs. Nathaniel Hawthorne wrote him a letter of thanks which is interesting because it shows the reaction of one discriminating reader to the story and is an example of the kind of sentiment and language rife at the time. "I do not believe," wrote Mrs. Hawthorne, "that in the English language there is anything more delicate, tender, arch, and spherical in rounded beauty. It is as ethereal as a snowflake, and as radiant as those rosy blossoms of the tropical plant which resemble snowflakes in form, as they tremble upon their cobwebby fibres and seem to the eye falling through the air. One seldom finds such sobriety and purity of composition. . . . If I abounded in means, I would bind it in purple velvet edged with diamonds and gild the leaves with solid gold."[2]

Few modern readers would be so lavish, but Mrs. Hawthorne was right about the "sobriety and purity of composition." She might have added restraint and economy. In its final form (Aldrich revised and polished his fiction as well as his poetry), the tale is given credibility by reference to Sir Charles Lyell (the father of modern geology) who was reputed to have examined the palm in 1846. Also Aldrich avoids responsibility for the truth of the legend by putting it in the mouth of a Miss Blondeau who had "the eyes and lips and Southern music to tell it with."[3]

Another story in "Peter Lynde's Sketch Book" shows signs of true Aldrich wit. "Miss Hepzibah's Lover" is the story of an old maid who is apparently being wooed by a wealthy, handsome young man. However, the young man is a sleepwalker and is actually doing his unusual wooing in sleep. He is engaged to a beautiful young woman who threatens to break the engagement when she discovers he is a sleepwalker: "I am sure I can't think of marrying a man who doesn't know when he is asleep!" But she did. And as for Miss Hepzibah, she consoles herself by thinking that her young man "was not so fast asleep as he appeared to be."

One has to agree with Fred Lewis Pattee that this story is "pure Aldrich" and that it "contains the essence of what he was to add to the short-story form: lightness of touch, wit, epigrammatic compression, and then a flash of suggestion that marks the end not an end at all but a beginning—in a word, art."[4]

"The Lady with the Balmoral," although it was never again printed, is also interesting to anyone who relishes Aldrich because it is the germ of the technique that was perfected in

"Marjorie Daw." The writing is immature and strained; for example: "I was vastly relieved when Mr. Markham at last retired to his own room to drown his restless soul, as he intimated, in the intoxicating bowl. The inebriating vessel so tragically alluded to was the bowl of his meerschaum pipe. In a few minutes such volumes of smoke came pouring through the keyhole of the door which separated our apartments that I rushed frantically into his chamber with a vague apprehension of finding him a mass of cinder." True, this is forced writing marred by overstatement, elegant variation, and a too-conscious striving for effect—faults which Aldrich was later able to correct.

The plot, however, is ingeniously handled. A Mr. Markham has fallen in love with a lady with a balmoral (a colored petticoat) whom he has seen but never met. He describes her so vividly to a friend that the friend also falls in love with her and decides to desert the girl he was engaged to, his Clementina. When he finally meets the lady with the balmoral, he discovers that she *is* his Clementina. This kind of plot was to be Aldrich's stock in trade. It has the elements in the raw of "Marjorie Daw."

Another early Aldrich story deserving mention is "A Young Desperado," published in the *Atlantic Monthly* (1867). Children, in early nineteenth-century American literature, were seldom, if ever, treated realistically. They were little saints, like Little Eva, who died in an exemplary fashion; little natural philosophers "trailing clouds of glory from Heaven"; little reformers who saved their drunken fathers from the saloons. Apparently none ever grew up, for few writers could resist the temptation to describe their deaths with tender, pious emotion. In a contemporary cartoon, one little boy, who has been reading magazine fiction, says to another, "I'm not going to be a good boy. Good boys always die." "A Young Desperado" is a sketch of a mischievous six-and-a-half-year-old character. When caught playing with matches, he carries on the following dialogue with his father:

> "Johnny," said I, in as severe a tone as one could use in addressing a person whose forehead glistened with syrup— "Johnny, don't you remember that I have always told you never to meddle with matches?"
>
> It was something delicious to see Johnny trying to remember. He cast one eye meditatively up to the ceiling, then he fixed it abstractedly on the canary bird, then he rubbed his ruffled brows with a sticky hand, but really for the life of him, he couldn't recall any injunctions concerning matches.
>
> "Well, Johnny, in order that you may not forget it in the future"—Here Johnny was seized with an idea. He interrupted me. "I'll tell you what you do, papa,—you just put it down in writing."[5]

The young desperado was not a bad boy in spite of the fact that he was the terror of the neighborhood. He was a completely believable character treated quite realistically. This kind of character has become common, but in 1867 it was a refreshing innovation that considerably brightened the pages of the staid *Atlantic Monthly*.

II *"Marjorie Daw" and Later Stories*

In 1837 Aldrich published a collection of his short stories under the title of *Marjorie Daw and Other People* that contained some of his best work. William Dean Howells was quick to recognize what others have since acknowledged: the collection almost created a new species in fiction, "a species in which character and incident constantly verge with us towards the brink of a quite precipitous surprise ending without being for a moment less delightful as character and incident, and without being less so even when we look up from the gulf into which they have plunged us."[6]

The title story, "Marjorie Daw," is a masterpiece of compression. Aldrich's method of composition was to write the last paragraph first; and, when the story was completed, he rigorously eliminated all but the essentials. In "Marjorie Daw" he gives us just enough detail to make Miss Daw live, and not one bit more. The story is told in an exchange of letters between two young men: one is suffering in the city with a broken leg; the other is at an isolated summer hotel where he has taken his father for his health. In their exchange of letters, the one in the country describes a beautiful colonial mansion across from his hotel and a lovely young girl, the only daughter of Colonel Daw, ex-banker and commander of a regiment during the Civil War. Miss Daw, as she swings in her hammock, sits on the piazza, or plays croquet on the lawn, is described with such exquisite skill that the young man in the city begins to fall in love with her. As his passion increases, the exchange of letters ends in a series of telegrams in which the city lover insists on coming to meet Miss Daw and his friend tries unsuccessfully to dissuade him. The lover finally arrives on the scene and is surprised by what he discovers, but no more so than the reader: Marjorie Daw was a figment of his friend's imagination.

The story won instant acclaim, an international reputation for the author, and is still anthologized. No one would claim that it is great literature (whatever that is), but it is artfully written, inventive, amusing, and mildly pitiful. There is nothing that will offend the taste of even the modern reader. In other words, it is a short story that will live and will continue to be read as long as readers enjoy an amusing, well-told tale.

Another Aldrich tale that is a masterpiece of its kind is "Two Bites at a Cherry," the title piece of a collection of short stories published in 1894. In the story, Marcus Whitelaw, a Henry James character without the sometimes boring subtlety of some of James's heroes, meets the woman who had rejected him fifteen years ago. They meet in a cathedral in Naples where they are among the throng waiting to see the miracle of the Liquefaction of the Blood of St. Jamarius. Before they actually speak, he sees her in the crowd: "a blond with the eyes of a brunette" and with "a rounded slenderness of figure which is one of our very best Americanisms" and fifteen years "had not touched the curve of the tall, slight figure." "Her clothing fitted closely," accentuating every line of the slender waist and "flower-like full bust."[7] She is, in a fact, a middle-aged Marjorie Daw. He recalls that her husband has died, and he hopes that perhaps his suit may be renewed. The suspense that the crowd feels waiting for the miracle to happen is made insignificant by the suspense the reader experiences as Marcus works his way through the crowd to speak to his old love. They finally meet and have a polite, sophisticated conversation that gradually leads to the overwhelming question and its devastating answer. Contrived, of course, but well done.

The remaining stories and sketches in the 1873 collection are, with one possible exception, not so skillfully handled as "Marjorie Daw." They were, however, better than most of the fiction published by the quality magazines of the time. Three of them, "A Rivermouth Romance," "Miss Mehetabel's Son," and "The Friend of My Youth," are local-color stories. Aldrich has not been given adequate attention as a local colorist, probably because the body of his work is small and his reputation as a poet overshadowed his short fiction. He did, however, leave some excellent local-color fiction in which he portrayed the town of Portsmouth as he remembered it. He knew the area well, loved it, and understood it. He grew to despise the dialect literature that filled the magazines of the 1870's and 1880's, but in "A Rivermouth Romance" he skillfully and unobtrusively uses the Irish brogue in parts of the dialogue. Rivermouth, obviously Portsmouth, was a quiet Puritan seacoast town most of the time. When the fleet came in, however, it became a little more lively. The story is based on the experience of Miss Margaret Callaghan, the trusted servant of one of the staid, modestly well-to-do families of Rivermouth who on her fortieth birthday secretly marries a drunken Irish sailor who is half her age. Like most of the local colorists, Aldrich fastened on a ludicrous or grotesque situation; but the setting is perfectly believable. In spite of some rather self-conscious writing and some slightly exaggerated incidents, the story is amusing; and the characters of Mr. and Mrs. Bilkins, the employers of Margaret, are well drawn.

Aldrich made good use one of the town's eccentrics in "A Friend of My Youth." The friend, who called himself Governor Dorr, was apparently an idle, wealthy character who had left Rivermouth as a boy and who had suddenly returned. He was kind, generous, and a great talker. His subject was usually literature, especially Shakespeare; but he was in reality a fraud, a gambler, an incurable ne'er-do-well who died friendless. Aldrich's more extensive treatment of his favorite town came later, but in these early stories he contributed, in a small way, to the growing local-color movement.

His ability to put grotesque characters in a realistic setting and his skill in contriving stories with surprise endings are neatly combined in "Miss Mehetabel's Son." The story takes place in an old tavern at Bayley's Four Corners in New Hampshire. The tavern had once been famous as a stopping point for the mail coach on the Great Northern Route, but the development of the railroad left it stranded. Now it had only one boarder, and Miss Mehetabel's son is, like Marjorie Daw, merely the product of his imagination. This story is a trifle but amusing.

In 1893 in *Two Bites at a Cherry, with Other Tales* Aldrich published a story that probes a little deeper into the life of Rivermouth. "For Bravery on the Field of Battle" is the story of James Dutton, a quiet, unimpressive young man who was nearly friendless in Rivermouth. No one understood why he enlisted in the army during the Mexican War, nor did anyone care. The town promptly forgot him after his departure until word came back that he had been decorated for saving a field piece and the life of his captain under heavy fire. He had also lost his leg. Of course, he became a hero overnight; and, when he arrived home, he was acclaimed enthusiastically. He was a cobbler by trade, and the town patronized his shop as it never had before. People stopped in to talk to him, to listen to his story, to admire his medal, and to read the inscription on it, "For Bravery on the Field of Battle."

But Dutton's good fortune did not last. As the town began to forget the war, never a popular one in Rivermouth anyway, the people began to forget Jimmy Dutton as well. It gradually became more convenient to patronize a shoe shop nearer by, and Jimmy was too proud to make it known that he was actually in want. He finally died on a cold winter night of starvation and exposure with his medal in his hand. Apparently he had died holding the medal before his eyes, for the frost from his breath so covered it that no one could read the inscription. Perhaps this ending is too climactic and contrived for modern taste, but it was carefully prepared for. As Dutton becomes more lonely and neglected, he, quite naturally, fell into the habit of gazing at his decoration and reminiscing over his faded glory.

The story itself is neatly told in a straightforward style. There is nothing morbid about it. In fact, it is handled with Aldrich's characteristic light touch and sense of humor. For example, Dutton's account of his action goes as follows:

> "The copper bullets were flying like hailstones, so it didn't much matter where a fellow went—he was sure to get peppered. Of course the captain couldn't be left up there, we wanted him for the morning parades. . . ."
>
> "I suppose you didn't leave your heart down there along with the senoriteers, did you Jemmy?" inquired a town Lovelace.

"No," said Dutton, always perfectly matter of fact; "I left my leg."

Ah, yes, life was very pleasant to him in those days!

Not only kindnesses, but honors were showered upon him. Parson Wibird Hawkins, in the course of an address before the Rivermouth Historical and Genealogical Society, that winter, paid an elegant tribute to "the glorious military career of our young Townsman"—which was no more than justice; for if a man who has a limb shot off in battle has not a touch of glory, then war is an imposition.[8]

And in explaining why Dutton did not have a pension, Aldrich pointed out that "at that conservative stage of our national progress, it was not possible for a man to obtain a pension simply because he happened to know the brother of a man who knew another man that had intended to go to war, and didn't. Dutton's claims, too, were seriously complicated by the fact that he had lost his discharge papers; so the matter dragged, and was still dragging when it ceased to be of any importance to anybody."[9]

Aldrich's perception is important because it is a perfectly realistic portrayal of human nature as it manifests itself in a small town. In contrast to Stephen Crane's savage denunciation of small-town people in "The Monster," Aldrich's "For Bravery on the Field of Battle" is realistic criticism of small-town life that can be bad but is not *all* bad. It is no more realistic to overemphasize evil than it is to ignore it. In Aldrich's story, a tragedy occurs; but Aldrich understood that tragedies often are caused by perfectly good, well-intentioned people. In "For Bravery on the Field of Battle," the town is not the villain. In fact, there is no villain at all; for "Thoughtless neglect, all the more bitter by contrast, had followed thoughtless admiration."[10] If Dutton's plight had been known, however, he would willingly have been given all kinds of assistance. The people of Rivermouth were good people, but such people can be cruel through thoughtlessness and neglect and still be good people. This story has something to say about human nature. Its meaning is simple, organic to the story, and true.

Another type of short fiction Aldrich handled very well might be called whimsical or fanciful Gothic. One of the most amusing, "A Struggle for Life," appears in the 1873 edition of *Marjorie Daw and Other People.* The story is based on a situation that would have delighted Poe: a young American is locked in a tomb in Paris next to the dead body of the girl he was engaged to marry. The tomb is ventilated, but it is damp and cold. Although he has a few matches, he has difficulty lighting them on the damp wall; but, when he succeeds in lighting one, he discovers that only one of the candles used in the funeral service had been left. He immediately lights it, inspects the walls and door of the tomb, and discovers that escape is impossible. He then extinguishes the candle, divides it in four equal parts, and plans to eat one each day. His thoughts, fears, and ravenous hunger are described graphically but economically. We suffer with him as he tries to estimate the lapse of time in the darkness of the tomb, as he struggles to fight off sleep, and as he conserves his precious pieces of candle. Anyone who has read very much of Aldrich's fiction would be prepared for a surprise ending, even to this gruesome situation; but this story has two. The young lover must be left in the tomb, however, to avoid spoiling the story for those who are curious about how he escaped. This much can be revealed—he did.

"The Chevalier de Resseguire" is another sketch that verges on the morbid. It is about a strong impulse that a literary man has to purchase a skull that he sees in the window of a queer bookshop. He purchases the skull, installs it in his library, and it is not difficult to imagine what the story would have been had Poe written it, but the following paragraph, which begins the sketch, sets the tone of the whole: "I am unable to explain the impulse that prompted me to purchase it. I had no use for a skull—excepting, of course the one I am temporarily occupying. There have been moments, indeed, when even that has seemed to me an encumbrance. Nevertheless, I bought another."[11]

The description of the bookstore that houses the skull and that sells only "works on phrenology, toxicology, evolution, mesmerism, spiritualism, and kindred occult sciences"[12] is sharply and artfully drawn:

> These thin, dingy octavos and twelvemos, . . . were chiefly of a psychical and social nature, and were no doubt daringly speculative. The patrons of the establishment shared its eccentricity . . . a half-shabby middle-aged man, who seemed a cross between a low comedian and a village undertaker; sometimes it was a German or a Pole, cadaverous, heavy-bearded, with a restlessness about the eyes—a fellow that might be suspected of carrying dynamite pellets in his waist-coat pocket; and sometimes it was an elderly female, severe of aspect, with short hair in dry autumnal curls, evidently a person with advanced views on Man, and so flat in figure, so wholly denuded of graceful feminine curves, as to make it difficult for one to determine, when she lingered an instant in the doorway, whether she was going in or coming out.[13]

The sketch is a dialogue between the skull and its new owner. Its original owner was the Chevalier de Resseguire whom the present owner knew since he had been writing an article on the political intrigues of the reigns of Louis XV and Louis XVI. The author also knew that the Chevalier "was an adventurer from Toulouse, pseudo man-of-letters, a sort of prowling epigram," and not a man to be trusted. After some amusing conversation, they get into a violent argument. The writer in his rage threatens to give the Chevalier a sound caning:

> "Monsieur forgets himself," said the Chevalier, and the Chevalier was quite right. "The rapier and the pistol are—or were—my weapons. Fortunately for monsieur I am obliged to say *were*. Monsieur can be impertinent with impunity."
>
> "I've a great mind to knock your head off!" I cried, again in the wrong.[14]

Of course it was a dream, a hackneyed device indeed; but the story is saved from pure banality by Aldrich's droll wit and skillful writing.

Another sketch in the same vein that shows Aldrich's taste for the macabre is "His Grace the Duke." The duke was Henry Grey, Duke of Suffolk, who was decapitated in 1554 "as a slight testimonial of Queen Mary's appreciation of the part he had played in Northumberland's conspiracy and some collateral enterprises." The head was preserved in the Church of the Holy Trinity in London and displayed to a few stray tourists, mostly American, with specialized tastes. Apparently Aldrich was among them, for certainly "His Grace the Duke" is the record of his own experience. Aldrich once remarked to Annie Fields that he had a "strange impression of having lived before—once in London especially—not at St. Paul's, or Pall Mall, or any of the great places where [he] might have been deceived by previous imagination—not at all,—but among some old streets where [he] had never been before and where [he] had no associations."[15]

Aldrich made use of this strong feeling in "His Grace the Duke" when he visited the Church of the Holy Trinity to see the relic:

> As I gazed upon the sharply cut features, I had that odd feeling, which has often come to me in cathedral towns in England, and especially during my walks through the older sections of old London—the impression of having once been a part of it all, as possibly I was, in some remote period. At this instant, with my very touch upon a tangible something of that haunting past—at this instant, I repeat, the gloomy church . . . and all of the life that is, slipped away from me, and I was standing on Tower Hill with a throng of other men-at-arms, keeping back the motley London rabble at the point of our halberds."

Aldrich then gives a vivid description of the execution of the Duke of Suffolk in which he is able to make the reader feel that he is seeing it firsthand: "The bitter morning on Tower Hill, the surging multitude, the headsman with his axe."[16]

To the spate of war stories that followed the Civil War, Aldrich added but little. However, he did make good use of his very brief war experience as a correspondent for the New York *Tribune*. One of his war stories, "Quite So," has some good descriptions of camp life that ring true, as does "The White Feather" which exploits the theme of father and son fighting on opposite sides. By far the best of his stories concerning the war, or rather its aftermath, is "My Cousin the Colonel" in which Aldrich drew on his memories of post-war New York City. Although the story is primarily a humorous portrait of a rogue, he creates an authentic glimpse of the burgeoning city as it was in the late 1860's: the heedless horsecars, the oyster saloons, the cafe concerts in the Bowery where the guests passed their evenings with lager beer, the city "strewed with shreds and patches of the war." Even the drivers and conductors of streetcars wore "overcoats made out of shoddy army blankets, and the dustmen went about in cast-off infantry caps."[17]

The characters are amusing. Mr. Wesley, the secretary of the insurance company, is a conservative, bookish, and above all patient, young man. His wife Clara used to say to him: "Wesley, you are not brilliant, but you are good." Clara is very much like her husband, but she has no patience at all about the war; she is a fanatic about the cause. As Mr. Wesley said, ". . . she never had a brother. If she had one, he would have been killed in the first battle of the war. She sent me to the front to be killed, and I went willingly; but I wasn't good enough; the enemy wouldn't have me at any price after a year's trial." The Wesley's children, Sheridan and Ulysses, are important only as they shed light on Mrs. Wesley's sentiments.

Mr. Wesley's only relative is Washington Flagg, born in Maine but a Southerner at heart. He is also a tramp, a liar, a drunkard, and a swindler; but, posing as a colonel (he never was in the war), he establishes himself temporarily in the Wesley household. The strained dinner conversations as the family tries to avoid any discussion of the war are the best part of the story. The colonel cannot keep quiet about the lost cause, and Clara's sharp tongue pierces the façade of her calm politeness in spite of herself. After the colonel has insulted his benefactors unpardonably and is asked to leave, he does; but later he swindles Mr. Wesley by imposing on the family connection again. When the hoax is discovered, Mrs. Wesley said, very gently, "Wesley, you were not brilliant, but you were good."

In *A Sea Turn and Other Matters* Aldrich published a story that is not in his usual vein. In "Shaw's Folly" he attempts to handle a social theme, but he does so without complete success. Aldrich, himself, had an ambivalent attitude toward the story. On the one hand he thought it the best long short story he had written since "Marjorie Daw,"[18] but he had apparently written slightingly of it to Sarah Orne Jewett. She replied: "You spoke slightingly of 'Shaw's Folly' but that was the folly of TBA. It is done with such freedom of hand and brightness of touch that I liked it most commonly well. . . . But I love the way you have written the story. There's realism seen from the humorous point of view. The trouble with most realism is that it isn't seen from any point of view at all and so its shadows fall in every direction and it fails of being art."[19]

Although the story is treated lightly and from a humorous point of view, it is also told from the point of view of a conservative thinker, albeit a kindly one. Shaw's folly was an experiment in helping the poor help themselves. Augustus Shaw, who had made a fortune in business, retired in the prime of his life so that he could enjoy life—"make visits, and give little dinners, and read what's-his-name's novels, and see something of the social world." He soon discovered, however, "that amusement as a permanent occupation was far from being a simple matter. In order to achieve even a moderate success in it, it is indispensable that one should have a long line of ancestors austerely trained in the art of doing nothing. Augustus Shaw could not comply with this requisition. He had come of plain New England people who believed in the gospel of toil, and had practiced it to the end. . . . He was the first of his race to withdraw from active life without the special intervention of Providence."[20]

To fend off boredom, Shaw purchased an apartment house which he put in good repair, hoping to rent it to the respectable, deserving poor—"the man and woman who would like to live cleanly lives in cleanly homes, but whose poverty condemned them to haunts of filth and darkness." He interviewed each prospective occupant with care, and he finally filled the apartment with "worthy and respectable families at a rental just sufficient to keep the premises in repair." The experiment failed. Some were tardy with their payments; some paid but rarely; one tenant turned out to be a bank robber.

Aldrich was vaguely aware of the fact that this kind of paternalism is likely to fail because it robs the poor of their self-respect. As Shaw contemplates the ruin of his model apartment, he muses: "Yet some man will do this thing some day, and make it pay. The idea was there all right, though I haven't seemed to know how to work it out. Perhaps there was too much charity in my plan—the kind of charity that gives birth to paupers." Although the plan was a failure, it was "one of those failures in which lie the seeds of success. . . . A dim and scarcely recognized presentiment of this was Mr. Shaw's sole consolation."

The story is also a failure because Aldrich's ideas were as vague as his characters. The story raises a problem, but the author has not thought the problem through. Most readers would agree with Sarah Orne Jewett who complained that "the only shadow of dissatisfaction that a fond reader can find is, that the writer didn't say what the cure might have been for such a sad failure!"[21] Aldrich could not because he really did not know.

One more story in *A Sea Turn and Other Matters* deserves mention. Although "The Case of Thomas Phipps" has a contrived plot and a surprise ending that hinges on the trite device of a will, it is nonetheless a good story. It is saved by the amusing character of Thomas Phipps, a rugged individualist in the best sense of the word. He is the adopted son of a wealthy deacon, his uncle, who plans that Tom will marry one of his daughters and manage the farm. But Tom "hated the business with great cheerfulness," and Tom's cheerfulness deceived his uncle who was astounded when Tom announced that he was not going to be a farmer but a house painter. The deacon was also angered, for he finally delivered an ultimatum: "Thomas Phipps, if that's your last word, I don't ever want to see you inside my house again!"

Tom never did go inside the house again but set up as a painter and married the postmaster's daughter who brought him no dowry at all. When the deacon drove by Tom's shop, Thomas would make him a friendly and respectful salutation, which was never returned. But Tom holds no grudge. "I'm not going to bow to Uncle Daniel just as long as there is anything left of both of us," he would say. "I know I disappointed him, but I don't see why he takes it so hard. With his gray colored sense of fun, I should think he'd be amused. I had to do what I did, or I wouldn't ever have been happy."

Tom and his wife have a hard time of it financially because Tom is a house painter with esthetic principles. He refuses to put the wrong color of paint on a house, and home owners dislike having their taste questioned. Tom is nearly destitute. When the deacon dies, he leaves Tom $1,000 on the condition that Tom will not attend the funeral. But Tom does attend, and explains to his wife: "Self-respect comes high, but it's the only thing that's worth what it costs—that and first-class linseed oil."

The story is really a little parable with mild satire on greed. No one in the town can understand Tom's actions. When the townspeople hear that Tom intends to attend the funeral, "the report was instantly credited. It was so like Tom Phipps to kick over his own pail of milk. It had been his chief occupation ever since he was five years old and dazzling success had crowned his efforts." That is the view of the town, but the reader knows that Tom, like Huck Finn, must obey his impulses and that they are right in every case if one thinks, unlike everyone in the town, that happiness and self-respect are more important than money.

"The Case of Thomas Phipps," like all of Aldrich's fiction, can be read with pleasure if it is not taken too seriously. For those who savor skillful writing for its own sake, and a quiet sense of humor, Aldrich's short fiction can be rewarding.

CHAPTER 4

The Novels

A LDRICH'S FIRST NOVEL, *Daisy's Necklace: And What Came of It* (1857) is an unpromising fledgling work, but it is interesting for the light it sheds on the taste of the readers of the nineteenth century. Aldrich's biographer, Ferris Greenslet, suggests it was started as a serious venture in popular novel writing and that Aldrich turned it into a burlesque as an afterthought. It is hard to believe that the following dialogue between a boy and girl ten years old could have been written seriously:

> "Bell," said the boy, "we never grow weary of looking at the sea."
> "No; because while we are watching, we think that father may be coming home to us across its bosom; and we count the waves as if they were moments. We like to see them roll away, and feel that time grows shorter between father and us."
> "Yes, that is so," he replied; "but then, we love night almost as much as the sea."
> "That is because we have a Father in heaven as well as one at sea," and the girl shaded her angel face with a dainty little hand.
> "And we love the sunbeams and the flowers, Bell!"
> "We do indeed!" cried Bell, and the sunshine nestled among her curls. "We do indeed! because God, like the good fairy in our story book, comes in sunlight, or hides in flowers; and he reveals himself in ever so many ways, to all who love him."

But whether Aldrich was seriously trying to write a popular novel or was parodying the form makes little difference now. No one but a literary historian will ever care to read it. It does, however, show us what the popular novel was like in Aldrich's day. It employs the standard devices: the lost will, the death of an angelic little girl, the lost father. The characters are also stereotypes: the Scrooge-like miser, the noble young man, and the faultless heroine. And the title is no more ridiculous than titles of some of the contemporary fiction that Aldrich satirizes—*Murdered Milkmaid, Bloody Hatchet, The Seducer's Victim, The Deranged Daughter, The Phantom of Philadelphia,* and other lurid titles created to cater to a morbid, inflamed taste.

But Aldrich did not use all of the devices of the sentimental novel. In the Epilogue, the author and a critic, Barescythe, discuss the book. The author admits he wrote the book to sell, but Barescythe points out that it won't because there are no sunsets described: "There should be one at the end of each chapter—twenty sunsets at least. Then you have no seduction. What modern novel is complete without one. It gives a spicy flavor to the story. People of propriety like it. Prim ladies of an uncertain age always dote on the gallant, gay lothario, and wish he wasn't so *very* wicked." And Barescythe continued, "there should be a dreadful duel, in which the hero is shot in his hyacinthine locks, falls mortally wounded, dripping all over with gory blood, and is borne to his lady love on a shutter!"

Barescythe was right. The novel sold about half of the first edition. The remaining half was sold to another publisher and was published with another novel of about the same size and caliber, *The Stain of Birth.*[1] Although Aldrich was indignant to see his book in such company, it probably deserved to be there.

I The Story of a Bad Boy

With the exception of *Out of His Head,* which can hardly be called a novel, Aldrich wrote no more novels until 1870 when he published his masterpiece, now a minor American classic, *The Story of a Bad Boy*. Admittedly autobiographical, this novel consists of Aldrich's memories of his childhood in New Orleans and in Portsmouth, New Hampshire, where its hero, Tom Bailey, is sent to complete his education. He lives in the home of his grandfather, Captain Nutter, a retired sea captain. The book is a series of episodes—at school, in the village, and on the Pisataqua River that flows past the village to the sea. There are fights in school, which Tom Bailey wins, of course; snowball battles; Fourth of July celebrations; and an amusing series of mischief-making pranks that earn Tom Bailey the title "bad boy"; but he is not such a very bad boy.

The book is pleasurable reading even today, but it is important for other reasons. As the first realistic treatment of an American boy, it had a positive influence on others who established the tradition of the boy story in American literature; and it was also an early contribution to the development of Realism. In the Preface to the 1894 edition of the novel, Aldrich explained why he chose his title: He "wished simply to draw a line at the start between his hero—a natural, actual boy—and that unwholesome and altogether improbable little prig which had hitherto been held up as an example to the young. The poet Wordsworth assisted by Plautus maintains—to the everlasting confusion of Mr. Darwin—that 'the good die first.' Perhaps this explains why the Bad Boy has survived so many good boys in the juvenile literature of the past two decades."

William Dean Howells, who was quick to recognize the novelty of the realistic treatment of boyhood, wrote in his review in *The Atlantic Monthly* (January, 1870): "No one else seems to have thought of telling the story of a boy's life, with so great desire to show what a boy's life is, and with so little purpose of teaching what it should be; certainly no one else has thought of doing this for the American boy!" Aldrich actually established the strong tradition of the boy in American literature that was carried on by Charles Dudley Warner, William Dean Howells, Mark Twain, Stephen Crane, and in the twentieth century by J. D. Salinger and a host of others.

The probable influence of *The Story of a Bad Boy* on Mark Twain, who began his lifelong friendship with Aldrich in 1871, has been pointed out by Walter Blair.[2] Tom Bailey, Aldrich's hero and narrator, anticipates Tom Sawyer; he has a dull time in Sunday School, sneaks out of his bedroom window for night-time adventures, imitates the heroes of books which he had read, camps with other boys on an island where they played they were Spanish sailors. Blair also points out the similarity between Aldrich's description of sentimental, first love-sickness and Twain's own treatment of the same theme in *Tom Sawyer*. And it was Aldrich and Clemens who showed Charles Dudley Warner and William Dean Howells the mine of literary material that lies in the memory of childhood experience.

Of course, Aldrich was not the first to use the local color of the New England village. Harriet Beecher Stowe's *The Pearl of Orr's Island* (1869) had preceded him; and Whittier, Lowell, and Hawthorne had used the New England scene and its history. But Hawthorne's use of the New England background is incidental, and Lowell's and Whittier's interest in it is sporadic. In an age when moralistic, sentimental, romantic tales were the vogue, Aldrich showed that it is possible to write interesting books simply by writing well about what he knew and loved—the town of his boyhood, Portsmouth, New Hampshire.

In *The Story of a Bad Boy*, we find no romantic adventure, no angelic little girls piously wasting away, no seduction, no wicked rakes, no diabolical villains—in Aldrich's words, none of the standard romantic appeals. With the exception of a highly unlikely incident—Tom invites to his home a wandering Irish sailor who amazingly turns out to be the long-lost husband of Kitty Collins, Grandfather Nutter's servant—things happen naturally in the novel.

In Rivermouth, life moves quietly and on the Sabbath grimly. Aldrich's account of the Puritan Sabbath is delightful. It begins at seven o'clock when Grandfather Nutter "comes smilelessly downstairs." Then the funereal atmosphere sets in and is maintained the rest of the day. Grandfather Nutter is "dressed in black, and looks as if he had lost all his friends during the night." Miss Abigail, his old maid sister, "also in black, looks as if she were prepared to bury them, and not indisposed to enjoy the ceremony." At breakfast "the coffee-urn—a solemn and sculpturesque urn at any time, but monumental now" is gazed on by Miss Abigail "as if it held the ashes of her ancestors." The meal is eaten in silence and is followed by Bible reading in the parlor, the Sabbath being one of the rare days the parlor is used. No light reading is allowed, nothing but Richard Baxter's *The Saints' Everlasting Rest*. Even the bluebottle fly "attempts to commit suicide by butting his head against the window."

Grandfather Nutter then inquires "in a sepulchral voice" if it is time for "Sabbath school." After Sabbath school is the meeting in which the Reverend Wibird Hawkins "holds out very little hope" of salvation to any of his congregation. After the meeting, the Nutter family has a "dead-cold dinner" that was "laid-out" the day before.

After the second Sabbath service later in the day, a long and tiresome one, Tom and his grandfather take a walk to "visit, appropriately enough, a neighboring graveyard." Aldrich tolerably concludes that there was no hypocrisy in the Puritan Sabbath: "It was merely the old Puritan austerity cropping out once a week. Many of these people [of Rivermouth] were pure Christians every day in the seven—excepting the seventh. Then they were decorous and solemn to the verge of moroseness."

Rivermouth came to life vigorously on occasion, however.

The Fourth of July was enthusiastically and dangerously celebrated. "Muskets, blunderbusses, and pistols were banging away lively all over town"; and Tom, not content with "setting off two packs of fire-crackers in an empty winecask," wanted "to add something respectable to the universal din." This he did by shooting a small, brass pistol which went off, to Tom's amazement, with a tremendous explosion and then disappeared in the air.

The official ceremony was colorful and cacophonous. The town square was "thronged by crowds of smartly dressed townsfolk and country folk; for Rivermouth on the Fourth was the centre of attraction to the inhabitants of the neighboring villages." And over on one side of the square were

> twenty or thirty booths arranged in a semicircle, gay with little flags and seductive with lemonade, ginger-beer, and seed-cakes. Here and there were tables at which could be purchased the smaller sort of fireworks; such as pinwheels, serpents, double-headers, and punk warranted not to go out. Many of the adjacent houses made a pretty display of bunting, and across each of the streets opening on the Square was an arch of spruce and evergreen, blossoming all over with patriotic mottoes and paper roses.

The celebration proper was "a noisy, merry bewildering scene" with an "incessant rattle of small arms, the booming of the twelve-pounder firing on the Mill Dam, and the silvery clangor of the churchbells ringing simultaneously—not to mention an ambitious brass band that was blowing itself to pieces on a balcony—."

But most of the time the boys of Rivermouth had to make their own fun. There were no Little League baseball teams, no Boy Scouts, no YMCA's, and other forms of adult-organized recreation. The adults of Rivermouth, as in most if not all nineteenth-century American towns, assumed responsibility for only the education and the moral instruction of their young people. If a boy sometimes found time heavy on his hands, he at least had the chance to develop his imagination and ingenuity in providing his own recreation.

And the boys of Rivermouth were imaginative and ingenious enough. They organized a dramatic production of *William Tell* in the Nutter barn that very nearly ended in disaster when William Tell missed the apple. And the boys of the Temple Grammar School—only twelve select ones—organized a secret society, the Rivermouth Centipedes. "Each of the elect wore a copper cent (some occult association being established between a cent apiece and a centipede!) suspended by a string around his neck." They had an elaborate initiation ceremony in which the candidate was led blindfolded to the Grotto of Enchantment where he was ordered to the brink of several precipices and "ordered to step over many dangerous chasms," all "accompanied by dismal groans from different parts of the grotto." Finally he was read the by-laws and the "penalties attached to the abject being who should reveal any of the secrets of the society." The society was not organized for any benevolent purpose. If it had any purpose at all, "it was to accomplish as a body the same amount of mischief" the boys "were sure to do as individuals."

But all boyhood escapades didn't end in innocent mischief. The boys were not always so fortunate. The river and the sea were a constant invitation and menace to the Rivermouth boys. Drownings were common, but the broad river with its abandoned wharves and rocky islands was too great a temptation for the boys to resist. And every Rivermouth boy

looked upon the sea as being in some way mixed up with his destiny. While he is yet a baby, lying in his cradle, he hears the dull far-off boom of the breakers; when he is older, he wanders by the sandy shore, watching the waves that come plunging up the beach like white-maned sea-horses, as Thoreau calls them; his eye follows the lessening sail as it fades into the blue horizon, and he burns for the time when he shall stand on the quarterdeck of his own ship, and go sailing proudly across that mysterious waste of waters.

And Tom, like all Rivermouth boys, yearned "to own the whole or a portion of a row-boat. . . ." He finally purchased one with three of his friends, Phil Adams, Fred Langdon, and Binny Wallace. At the earliest opportunity they loaded their new boat, the *Dolphin*, with supplies for "an excursion to Sandpeep Island, the last of the islands in the harbor." After the four boys had landed and cooked their feast of cod chowder, cunners, and clams, they explored the island, played ducks and drakes, and went bathing. By this time the breeze had freshened, and "a muffled moan from the breakers" hinted of a storm. When Binny Wallace went to get supplies from the boat, the other boys soon heard cries of distress; rushing to the shore, they discovered Binny Wallace drifting out to sea without an oar. Because the breakers were so threatening, Binny knew, and his friends knew, that "the stoutest swimmer could not live forty seconds in those angry waters." The feeling of hopelessness they all had is best expressed in Tom's own words: "The sky grew darker and darker. It was only by straining our eyes through the unnatural twilight that we could keep the *Dolphin* in sight. The figure of Binny Wallace was no longer visible for the boat itself had dwindled to a mere white dot on the black water. Now we lost it, and our hearts stopped throbbing; and now the speck appeared again, for an instant, on the crest of a high wave." Then "finally it went out like a spark, and we saw it no more. Then we gazed at each other and dared not speak."

When the realistic account of the tragic death of Binny Wallace is compared with the romantic, sentimental, thoroughly improbable death of little Bell in *Daisy's Necklace*, it becomes apparent that Aldrich has learned to restrain his tendency to sentimentality and fine writing. But *The Story of a Bad Boy* has its limitations. The plot is episodic. Moreover, the various incidents it presents could be arranged in an entirely different order without appreciably damaging the book. Aldrich never learned to handle long plots skillfully, and there is in *The Story of a Bad Boy* no sustained suspense and no real, effective climax. Each incident in the life of Tom Bailey is complete in itself.

By and large the novel is superficial, but it was not intended to be an analytical probing into the life of the community. There is little or no criticism of social life implicitly or explicitly stated. There are, for example, second-class citizens in the town—the Irish servants and the boys who do not go to Temple Grammar School; but Aldrich is not concerned with their problems and writes from the point of view of the respectable middle class. Nor is there an evaluation of the social forces that determine the character of the townspeople. Like the local colorists, Aldrich was more concerned with the picturesque than with social analysis.

While *The Story of a Bad Boy* is a realistic treatment of boys and of their activities, it is not, like *Huckleberry Finn*, written from a boy's point of view. The narrator is an adult remembering the exploits of his youth; and there is, therefore, no serious conflict between Tom Bailey and the adult world. Tom is a boy who never skips school; and, while he does sometimes disobey and while his mischief does get him into conflict with the authorities, he always accepts the justice of his punishment, just as an adult looking back on his boyhood is inclined to do. However, if Aldrich had really attempted to enter the mind of Tom Bailey and to show us how a boy really thinks, the novel would have been a better book, or at least a different one.

What Aldrich does tell us about boys is true. In his chapter "A Frog He Would a-Wooing Go," he tells about his first love and about Nellie Glentworth, the girl he loved: "Nellie was at least five years my senior. But what of that? Adam is the only man I ever heard of who did not in early youth fall in love with a woman older than himself, and I am convinced that he would have done so if he had had the opportunity."

He recalls his misery: he was "wretched away from her, and only less wretched in her presence." His love affected his school work. He "went down in his Latin class at the rate of three boys a day." He knew that Nellie considered him a little boy, and it made him despise little boys and especially "one particular little boy—too little to be loved."

Aldrich treats this incident seriously because young Tom's sorrow was "genuine and bitter." "It is a great mistake," comments Aldrich, from his adult vantage-point, "on the part of elderly ladies, male and female, to tell a child that he is seeing his happiest days. . . . The burdens of childhood are as hard to bear as the crosses that weigh us down later in life, while the happinesses of childhood are tame compared with those of our maturer years."

But Aldrich, though sympathetic with Tom Bailey while he was genuinely stricken with his first love, was ready to laugh at the amusing figure Tom cut when he took it into his head "to be a Blighted Being." Although Tom "had an excellent appetite" and "liked society and out-of-door sports," he found "all these things "incompatible with the doleful character" he was about to assume. He neglected his clothing and his hair, he read "the more turgid poems of the late Lord Byron—'Fare thee well, and if forever,' etc." He also read "The Mysteries of Udolpho, by the amiable Mrs. Radcliffe." A translation of The Sorrows of Werther fell into his hands, and he recalled: "if I could have committed suicide without killing myself, I should certainly have done so."

Although Tom rather enjoyed being a "Blighted Being," a boy of his temperament could not maintain the role "longer than three consecutive weeks." Moreover, certain events occur which mature him rapidly. The most important one is the news of the death of his father. Although Aldrich's own father died before Aldrich went to live in Portsmouth, Tom Bailey's father of the novel dies just before Tom leaves Rivermouth. It was obviously Aldrich's purpose in rearranging the events in his life to show the difference between imaginary sorrow and real grief. Thus the "Blighted Being" chapter, which follows the departure of his first love, contrasts with the chapter that describes his genuine grief. The episode in which Tom's grandfather gives him the letter is best told in Aldrich's own words in a passage notable for its simplicity and restraint:

> My grandfather held the letter a few seconds irresolutely, and then commenced reading it aloud; but he could get no further than the date.
> "I can't read it, Tom," said the old gentleman, breaking. "I thought I could."
> He handed it to me. I took the letter mechanically, and hurried away with it to my little room, where I had passed so many happy hours.
> The week that followed the receipt of this letter is nearly a blank in my memory. I remember that the days appeared endless; that at times I could not realize the misfortune that had befallen us, and my heart upbraided me for not feeling a deeper grief; that a full sense of my loss would now and then sweep over me like an inspiration, and I would steal away to my chamber or wander forlornly about the gardens. I remember this, but little more.

The other characters in the novel are treated superficially, but they are presented with just enough detail to make them credible and individual. Captain Nutter, with his stern Puritan exterior, is a strict disciplinarian, but a tender-hearted one. Aunt Abigail has a remedy for every known ailment—hot drops—which she administers for everything from broken bones to running noses. Fat Pepper Whitcomb, Tom's chum, is practical but bubbles "over with sympathy for anyone in any kind of trouble." And there are many minor characters: Dame Jocelyn, Silas Trefethen, the Reverend Wibird Hawkins, and Mr. Grimshaw who are characterized briefly but effectively.

Of course many of the characters in the novel (the old-maid aunt, the eccentric minister, the kind schoolteacher) and many of the incidents (the fight with the bully, the escape out the bedroom window, the amateur theatrical) seem hackneyed and stereotyped to the modern reader. In fairness to Aldrich, however, it should be remembered that they were not so in his day. He must be given credit, therefore, for showing that ordinary people doing commonplace things can be interesting literary material.

II Prudence Palfrey

In *Prudence Palfrey*, his second novel, Aldrich attempted with limited success to construct a plot. It is concerned with the question: will John Dent return to Rivermouth from his expedition to the West in time to prevent the Reverend Mr. Dillingham, the new minister (who is really an impostor), from marrying the girl Dent loves, Prudence Palfrey? He does, and the novel ends with an absurd surprise ending. Coincidence and again a misplaced will are used to make the plot come out right. Moreover, the device of suspending the action to pick up a different thread of the story is annoyingly used.

However, the novel is saved in part by Aldrich's two literary talents: his wit and his accurate depiction of New England character. William Dean Howells, reviewing the novel in the *Atlantic Monthly*, claimed that "nothing wittier" had been written "in this country if we except three books of Dr. Holmes." Aldrich's wit is mild. Unlike the novels of Mark Twain, *Prudence Palfrey* hardly induces much more than a smile or chuckle, even with Aldrich's favorite device, the use of literary and Biblical allusion to describe ordinary things. "All Miss Palfrey's domestic laws" are described as "the law of the Medes and Persians, which altereth not." The "furtive glances of shyness and reverence" bestowed on the new minister by the belles of Rivermouth are likened to "the songs of the sirens." The countless hand-made slippers they sent to him "overran Mr. Dillingham's bedroom like the swarms of locusts that settled upon Egypt."

Sometimes Aldrich resorts to the ludicrous for his humor. The Honorable Sam Knubley observed of the new minister: "You can see with half an eye that he belongs to the Southern aristocracy, but he isn't eternally shinning up his genealogical tree. There's old Blydenburgh who is always perching himself on the upper branches and hurling down the cocoanuts of his ancestors at common folks."

On occasion Aldrich makes effective use of understatement. Although the Honorable Sam Knubley professes democratic sentiments, "It is not to be supposed that the Honorable Sam Knubley himself would have objected to a few brilliant ancestors." Likewise, Aldrich uses overstatement for his humorous effect. Again on the ancestral theme, he recalls: "I have encountered two or three young gentlemen in the capital of the Commonwealth of Massachusetts who seemed to have the idea that *they* were killed at the battle of Bunker Hill."

Aldrich's wit is never bitter. The above mild satire on New England ancestor worship is about as caustic as he cared to be. His wit does brighten his pages, however, so that, while his novels may be clumsy and superficial, they are never really dull.

Two incidents in *Prudence Palfrey* bear out his ability to delineate regional character. One is the dismissal of the old minister, Parson Wibird Hawkins, and the second, the arrival of the new one, the Reverend James Dillingham. Parson Wibird Hawkins insists in "remaining on the stage" too long, a not uncommon occasion in New England when ministers were noted for their devotion to their Master's work. But how does a congregation go about telling a man who has "christened them and married them and buried them" for fifty years, that he "is no longer wanted." This task is assigned to Deacon Wendell and Deacon Twombly. At first the Parson does not grasp the import of the deacons' message. Even when they bluntly suggest "the expediency of his retirement from active parochial duties," he does not understand. He thinks his congregation is merely concerned about his health and that it is "proposing a vacation to him":

> The parson persisted in not understanding the drift of the deacons' proposition until, at last, they were forced to use the most explicit language. . . . But when, finally, he was made to comprehend the astounding fact that the Old Brick Church of Rivermouth actually wished him to relinquish his pastorate, then the aged clergyman bowed his head, and, waving his hands in a sort of benediction over the two deacons, retreated slowly, with his chin on his breast, into a little room adjoining the study, leaving the pillars of the church standing rather awkwardly in the middle of the apartment.

The last sentence of the above is characteristic of Aldrich's method of tempering the pathetic with a mild bit of humor, a trick he may have learned from Holmes.

A more pleasant occasion in a New England village is the arrival of a new minister, especially a young and handsome one and especially in a town like Rivermouth "where almost literally nothing happens." On the Sabbath that the Reverend Mr. Dillingham is to preach his first sermon, there is an "unwonted, eager look on the faces of the neatly dressed throng" that had "crowded the streets at the earliest stroke of the bells." There is a "sort of pious Fourth-of-July" atmosphere in spite of the "fleecy, low-hanging clouds" that threaten rain.

When the new minister finally takes his place on the pulpit, "a contagious ripple and flutter . . . passed over the congregation. . . ." And "quick, subtle glances, indicative of surprise and approval, were shot from pew to pew." After the service, there are the inevitable opinions about it, but the people are more concerned with the new parson's "delicious" voice and "spiritual face" than with the content of the sermon. One member does remark that the sermon was "certainly an improvement on the poor old parson's interminable ninthlies and finallies."

Aldrich was able to capture the excitement and color of an occasion which seems rather strange to the modern reader unless he remembers that in those days the church was the center of the community. New Englanders, especially, took their religion seriously; and they attended long religious services regularly. Thus the choosing of a new minister was of considerable importance. Furthermore, a good sermon could be a welcome diversion to a people who lacked any form of mass entertainment. The intense interest in church affairs that was prevalent in the nineteenth century is no longer with us, and *Prudence Palfrey* is of some value for its pictures of an age that is gone.

III   The Queen of Sheba

Like *Prudence Palfrey*, Aldrich's next novel, *The Queen of Sheba*, is interesting only in parts. Aldrich correctly named it "a picturesque story, with very little incident and only a few characters."[3] The story begins when Mr. Edward Lynde, the young assistant cashier of a Rivermouth bank, rides out of town on a rented horse for a three weeks' horseback tour of northern New Hampshire. And this first chapter, "Mary," is straightforward and thoroughly delightful. Mary, Lynde's horse, is probably the most interesting character in the book. She is a "gaunt bony mare" he has rented from Deacon Twombly who says at the time: "Mary ain't what you'd call a racer . . . I don't say she is, but she's easy on the back." "Yellow in tint" and "of the texture of a hair-trunk," her most remarkable characteristic is an uncontrollable urge to back up. Lynde discovers that Deacon Twombly has a sense of humor when Mary, "At the end of two miles . . . stopped short and began backing, deliberately, and systematically, as if to slow music in a circus." "She continued to back, slowly

and with a certain grace that could have come only of confirmed habit" until Lynde is faced with the mortifying
prospect of returning to Rivermouth backwards.

Lynde's efforts to reverse his progress seem like a farce
to a twentieth-century generation whose only knowledge of
horses is from "Westerns." But, Aldrich explains, "Perhaps
nothing gives you so acute a sense of helplessness as to have
a horse back with you, under the saddle or between shafts.
The reins lie limp in your hands, as if detached from the
animal; it is impossible to check him or force him forward;
to turn around is to confess yourself conquered; to descend
and take him by the head is an act of pusillanimity. Of course
there is only one thing to be done; but if you know what
that is you possess a singular advantage over your fellow
creatures." After Lynde finally rights Mary, he continues his
journey. As he rides on, we are treated to some keenly
observant descriptions of Rivermouth in the early morning
before "anyone worth mentioning is up" and of the New
Hampshire countryside and mountains.

The second chapter is an annoying interruption of the
narrative; in it Aldrich sketches the history of Lynde. The
tale picks up again with a continuation of Lynde's journey.
After being unhorsed and after losing Mary, who started back
to Rivermouth at her top speed of four miles an hour, Lynde
discovers he is near a town and an adjacent insane asylum.
All of the inmates have escaped; and, unaware of this
occurrence he meets some of them on the road. Among them
is a beautiful young girl who calls herself "The Queen of
Sheba." After Mary is recovered, Lynde, touched by the sadness of the case of the deranged girl, ends his vacation: "He
had gone in search of the picturesque and the peculiar; he
had found them—and he wished he had not."

The New Hampshire chapters, while verging on the
burlesque at times, are saved by Aldrich's restraint and skillful writing. The remaining chapters take place in Europe

where Lynde has met and fallen in love with a girl who looks exactly like "The Queen of Sheba." But is she? After five chapters, interminable conversations, and some good descriptions of the oft-described Alps, it is discovered that it *is* she (completely cured, of course). She consents to marry Lynde. "And here our story ends—at the very point . . . where life began for those two."

The last half of *The Queen of Sheba* is beneath criticism. Not even Aldrich's wit and skill could sustain such an obvious, ill-conceived plot. The first part, however, contains some of Aldrich's most entertaining prose.

IV The Stillwater Tragedy

The Stillwater Tragedy, Aldrich's final novel, was a failure. It was a deliberate attempt to win critical favor, for Aldrich wrote to his friend, the poet-critic E. C. Stedman: ". . . am three chapters deep in a novel of different cast from any fiction I have attempted lately. Tragedy this time. I have observed that the writer of comedy, however artistic he may be, is thought less of than the dull fellow who does something sombre, badly. I am going to get my humor a suit of sables."[4]

The Stillwater Tragedy is far from tragedy; it is nothing more than an unfortunate combination of detective and labor novel. And Aldrich had not the skill, the experience, or the temperament to write either. Although the novel has some fairly good realistic descriptions of a New England manufacturing town, they are not enough to sustain the book.

The novel begins as a murder mystery when Lemuel Shackford, Stillwater's miser, is discovered murdered. The reactions of the town are well handled, and the arrival of the detective from a large city is convincing. But the detective theme is dropped while the affairs of Richard Shackford, the murdered man's cousin, and the general strike are presented. By the time the strike has been settled, the reader has lost interest in the murder; moreover, the novel closes with the solution of the crime which has but little connection with the more important labor dispute. A writer of detective fiction must have, above all, the ability to handle extended, complicated plot; and this Aldrich could never do.

Furthermore, Aldrich's experience with the laboring class was practically nonexistent. Aside from his brief mercantile experience in his uncle's countinghouse in New York City, he had deliberately cultivated only literary and artistic friendships, both in New York and in Boston. As a result, his laborers and their leaders in *The Stillwater Tragedy* are unconvincing.

And Aldrich's conservative attitudes and temperament made it difficult, if not impossible, for him to write a labor novel. He was far from a reformer. He honestly tried to be fair to labor but he could not. He admits in the novel that in one industry in Stillwater the workers are underpaid and are justified in striking. But he does not choose to write about that industry. He admits that some workers have been prudent, have saved money, and have not used the strike as an excuse for a drunken celebration; but he chooses to write about the barroom demagogues, the union agitators, and the vandals. When he is appalled that the Marble Workers' Association attempts to control the labor market by limiting the number of apprentices that the Slocum Marble Yard can hire, Aldrich shows that he has little understanding of how a union maintains its power. In fact, his anti-union attitude emerges because he obviously approves the action of Richard Shackford, who becomes manager of the Marble Yard, when Shackford demands, after the strike has been broken, that he be allowed to hire unlimited apprentices.

Aldrich's admitted prejudice against foreigners, as well as labor, is also apparent. Durgin, one of the marble workers who is actually a labor spy, speaks with hatred of Torrini, a labor agitator: "There was never any trouble to speak of among the tracks in Stillwater till he and two or three others came here with foreign grievances. These men get three times the pay they ever received in their own land and are treated like human beings for the first time in their lives. But what do they do? They squander a quarter of their week's wages at the tavern . . . and make windy speeches at the Union." Aldrich could not believe that there was such a person as an honest, intelligent, native-born labor leader.

After *The Stillwater Tragedy,* Aldrich wrote no more novels. It can be said of his fiction in general that he was at his best when his humor was "out of its sable shroud." With the exception of his last novel, he confined himself wisely to the things he knew best: New York City, Boston, and Portsmouth. He was out of his element when he tried "tragedy." In his novels and short fiction there is little or no violence, with the exception of the fight with the bully in *The Story of a Bad Boy;* there is sometimes pathos, as in the death of Parson Wibird Hawkins; sometimes tragedy, as in the death of Binny Wallace; but no real evil. Aldrich's villains, if they can be called such, are—with the exception of Jeff Sargin, the murderer in *The Stillwater Tragedy*—at worst misers or irresponsible rogues.

The strongest that can be said of his other characters and their actions is that sometimes they are mistaken. His women are all good and faithful. He does not deal with unpleasant domestic situations. Adultery, seduction, rape, poverty, and all of the darker problems and passions of man are not his concern.

However, although he is seldom profound and probing, he can be read and enjoyed today by those who still appreciate a charming wit; clear, economic prose; and the ability to handle short plots and incidents with great skill. If we take him for what he is—an amused, observant recorder of a limited section of life—and if we do not demand that he be something he never intended to be—a philosopher, a social crusader, or a teacher—he still has much to offer.

CHAPTER 5

Critical Theory

ASIDE from his charming essay about Herrick and his less
appreciative one about Emily Dickinson, Aldrich wrote
little criticism. Although he did not formulate a critical theory
in any single published work, he did have a critical theory
which he exercised as editor of the *Atlantic* from 1881 to
1890 and which served to guide his own creative work,
especially his poetry. But to find it one must piece it together
from his letters, his poetry, and the notes which he published
in 1904 in *Ponkapog Papers*. Such an examination reveals
that Aldrich, in his maturity, was not a Romanticist nor a
Realist; for the most part he had a clearly defined Classical
theory of literature.

After the Civil War the trend in American letters was from
Romanticism and New England Transcendentalism toward
Realism. While the New England writers lived on, their voices
became weaker and their ideals, in a diluted and sentimental
form, were carried on by the New York "genteel school" of
Bayard Taylor, E. C. Stedman, and others. The other camp,
the Realists, was led by Howells, Garland, Clemens, and
Crane. It has too often been assumed that a writer of the
1870's and 1880's either cast his lot with the old order or
embraced the new. There was, however, another alternative—
Classicism—and this is the one Aldrich chose.

It is true he was strongly influenced by the New York
"genteel school" during his poetic apprenticeship. The ideals

of this school were for the most part decadent Romanticisms as contrasted to the pre-war Boston literary culture. The Bostonian literary culture was not an isolated one; the Brahmins of Boston included politicians, scientists, teachers, and philosophers. The proximity of Harvard was a distinct advantage to them since it attracted scholars and leaders to the area, thus enriching the intellectual atmosphere immeasurably. With the possible exception of Longfellow, the poets, novelists, and essayists were very much men of their time with keen interests in science, politics, religion, and literature.

However, the post-war genteel circle, finding themselves in the Gilded Age of post-war materialism and in an atmosphere unsympathetic to the arts, turned inward. The Bayard Taylor circle in New York was composed almost exclusively of poets, artists, and actors. Lacking a sympathetic popular audience, they formed a mutual admiration society in which they upheld the ideals of the old generation as they understood them. While the English and American Romantic poets of an earlier age used themes from the past, they did not use them solely as a retreat from the present. The genteel writers, on the other hand, chose rather the distant in time and space for their musings with very little regard for the present at all. The earlier Romantics were, at least for one stage of theirs careers, revolutionary; the later genteel Romantics consistently opposed change.

Of course, the importance of the emotions plays an important part in any Romantic credo. But in the genteel writers, allowable sentiment becomes rapid gushings about the divinity of poetry, the dedication to the Muse, the pain of the soul. They turned from nature to books, from philosophy to sentimentality, from inspiration to mere facility, from Wordsworth and Coleridge to Tennyson.

While Aldrich was in New York, he shared the tender sentiments of the charmed circle at Tenth Street where the genteel writers met. He shared their enthusiasm for Tennyson, and he spoke freely of the soul, a habit he soon outgrew. In a letter to William Winter in 1855 he wrote of Tennyson: "I worship his books. There is one little song of his that haunts me. . . . It is 'The Miller's Daughter.' Is not that poem perfect?" And again in the same letter he wrote: "'The Princess' is a masterpiece. The man that fails to appreciate it must have very little soul."[1] He joined the mutual admiration society, enthusiastically writing to R. H. Stoddard in 1860: "When Longfellow and Bryant get brought down to their proper niches and you are carried up to yours and Boker is acknowledged to be a splendid dramatist then there will be a chance for me with my innumerable little songs about nothing in particular."[2] He shared their enthusiasm for the New England poets, and especially for Longfellow, whose poetry was to him "dearer than fine gold."[3] He also retreated to the medieval past and to the Orient for the subject matter for his poetry, for the most part ignoring contemporary life.

But Aldrich's natural New England reticence, his Bohemian wit, his sense of humor, and his common sense saved him from the excesses of the genteel set. His Oriental poetry became sportive in "When the Sultan Goes to Ispahan" and he spoofed the genteel writers' habit of addressing their Muse in his "Thalia," a poem in which a "middle-aged lyrical poet is supposed to be taking final leave of the Muse of Comedy":

> Some Melpomene woo,
>   some hold Clio the nearest;
> You, sweet Comedy—you
>   were ever sweetest and dearest!
>
> Nay, it is time to go.
>   When writing our tragic sister
> Say to that child of woe
>   how sorry I was I missed her.[4]

Although Aldrich remained on warm friendly terms with E. C. Stedman and Bayard Taylor, he saw much less of them and the rest of the genteel circle after he left New York City. And his poetry and his critical evaluations began to take on a more individual style, a style more closely allied to the seventeenth-century English poets and to the nineteenth-century French poets than to the German Romantics fostered by Bayard Taylor.

But as the Realist movement developed, Aldrich could not go all the way toward Realism despite his friend William Dean Howells. He considered himself a Realist in a sense. He is reported to have said of Howells: "Well I love him and even if I do not altogether agree with his views of literature. And yet, I am a believer in realism too. But there are kinds of realism I have no sympathy for."[5]

I *A Limited Realist*

Aldrich was a Realist in a limited way, if Realism means fidelity to region and character. He is not a Realist if Realism demands a true balancing of good and evil, vice and virtue, success and failure. He did not consider literature a fit subject for the unpleasant and commonplace. In his poem "At the Funeral of A Minor Poet," he complains that

> The mighty Zolaistic Movement now
> Engrosses us—a miasmatic breath
> Blown from the slums. We paint life as it is,
> The hideous side of it, with careful pains,
> Making a god of the dull Commonplace.[6]

Not only did he consider Realism unpleasant, he also thought it dull. "In nine cases out of ten," he wrote, "an exact reproduction of real life would prove tedious. Facts are not necessarily valuable, and frequently add nothing to fiction. The art of the realistic novelist sometimes seems akin to that of the Chinese tailor who perpetuated the old patch on the new trousers. True art selects and paraphrases, but seldom gives a verbatim translation."[7]

Imagination, according to Aldrich, is essential to literature; he wrote, "I like to have a thing suggested rather than told in full. When every detail is given, the mind rests satisfied, and the imagination loses the desire to use its own wings. The partly draped statue has a charm which the nude lacks. Who would have those marble folds slip from the raised knee of the Venus of Melas? Hawthorne knew how to make his lovely thought lovelier by sometimes half veiling it."[8]

Aldrich firmly believed that whatever thought literature should contain should be made lovely. In reviewing William Young's poem, "Wishmakers' Town," he regretted that it had "not escaped the *maladie du siècle*. The doubt and pessimism that marked the end of the nineteenth century find a voice in the bell-like strophes with which the volume closes. It is the dramatist rather than the poet who speaks here. The real message of the poet to mankind is ever one of hope. Amid the problems that perplex and discourage, it is for him to sing 'Of what the world shall be / When the years have died away.' "[9]

The pessimism of the age touched him, but not because he was shallowly optimistic. His poem "The Shipman's Tale" expresses what many felt after the impact of science on the nineteenth-century religious beliefs. It seemed that the world (the ship) was, as Stephen Crane wrote, aimlessly drifting; or, as Aldrich thought, it headed for total destruction. But Aldrich regretted that he had written "The Shipman's Tale," for he believed that if poetry should carry any message at all, it should be a hopeful one. In his charming essay on Herrick he noted: "It sometimes happens that the light love-song reaching few or no ears at its first singing, outlasts the seemingly more prosperous ode which, dealing with some passing phase of thought, social or political, gains the instant applause of the multitude."[10] A poem could be serious but need not be concerned with " 'tears from the depth of some divine despair' " and "probings into the tragic heart of man."

"Nearly all true poets," Aldrich thought, "have been whole-some and joyous singers. A pessimistic poet, like the poisonous ivy, is one of nature's sarcasms."[11] Thus Aldrich was not "genteel," Romantic, nor Realist. When he broke with the New York school, he continued to use the subject matter of the Romantics, but his method of treatment became more and more Classical.

II *Critic of Poetry*

As editor of *The Atlantic Monthly* from 1881 to 1890, he was a severe critic and, of the poetry that was submitted, an exacting one. He read all the poetry that came into his office with a poet-critic's trained eye and "even the single felicity of phrase or graceful thought in a poor poem never escaped his notice."[12] But his standards were exacting. In a letter to his friend and fellow poet, E. C. Stedman, he complained: "You are the only one of our day and generation who is doing anything at present. In your letter you speak of having written two poems. I wish you'd send them to me. I am slowly making up my mind to publish none but incontestably fine poems in the 'Atlantic'—which means only about four poems per year. . . . If you could see the piles of bosh sent to this office you'd be sick at heart."[13]

Aldrich was in fact a purist in the matter of English usage. "To his fastidious sense of phrase and syntax, reading proof was a sacrament," his assistant, Miss S. M. Francis, recalled; "and it fared ill with any split infinitive or suspended nomina-tive—even with such seemingly innocent locutions as 'several people'—that fell under his searching eye."[14] Although Aldrich was not a crusading editor, he was an extremely competent one; and under his editorship *The Atlantic Monthly* "won its international reputation as being, in the words of an English review, 'the best edited magazine in the English language.' "[15]

If a severe critic of the poetry of others, he was even

severer of his own. He must have had Walt Whitman in mind
when he wrote

> Great thoughts in crude unshapely verse set forth,
> Lost half their preciousness, and ever must,
> Unless the Diamond with its own rich dust
> Be cut and polished, it seems little worth.

And in a paragraph on Richard Lovelace, he wrote, "A little
thing may be perfect, but perfection is not a little thing," and
a trifle " 'no bigger than an agate stone on the forefinger of
an alderman' shall outlast the Pyramids. The world will have
forgotten all the great masterpieces of literature when it for-
gets Lovelace's three verses to Lucasta on his going to the
wars. More durable than marble or bronze are the words, 'I
could not love thee, deare, so much, loved I not honor
more.' "[16] This demand for high polish and perfection Aldrich
applied fastidiously to his own poetry. In 1896 he wrote to
Frank Dempster Sherman berating him for what Aldrich considered undeserved praise for his verses: "As for myself," he
wrote, "I confess that I am often discouraged. The poem I
had in mind and the poem I find after it has cooled off on
paper are such different things. I have written only two or
three things of which I am not wholly ashamed."[17] And again
he wrote to Sherman, regretting his own early poetry: "I
would like to be young again just in order not to write those
old verses. . . . Why doesn't a poet have his art and his impulse at once."[18]

He composed slowly and with painstaking care, often keep-
ing a short poem on his desk for weeks before releasing it to
his publisher. Admiring precise diction, he searched the
language for the right word; and he once tried every possible
word in the language to describe the cry of the sea gull before finally deciding on "petulant."

Prominent also in the Classicist's literary credo is the demand not only for perfection but also for clarity. Aldrich

could not tolerate obscurity of thought. Early in his career he wrote to his fiancée, Miss Woodman, asking her to read his manuscript, "Judith and Holofernes." "See if there are not any passages," he wrote, "where the idea is not worked out sharply. Obscurity, I think, is a kind of stupidity, and I seek to avoid it always."[19]

He recognized that some beautiful but elusive feelings and thoughts are fit subjects for poetry but probably cannot be perfectly expressed. In a letter to William Winter, commenting on the poetry of Philip J. Bailey, he wrote:

> There are many verses famous among men of letters (I do not refer to Bailey's particularly) which, to the mere matter of fact reader, seem downright dullness; yet an indescribable beauty runs through them that cannot be analyzed; it can only be *felt*. Such verses I am not slow to love and praise; but many of Bailey's lines have to be turned, and fingered and taken apart like a Chinese puzzle, to get at their meaning, and then, like the puzzle, they are not worth the trouble. This, I think, is a serious fault, and too general among our noblest poets.[20]

Little wonder that Aldrich thought Donne's poems "grotesquely indigestible" and found Browning only partially satisfactory. He wrote to Stedman: "When he [Browning] did not crawl in the slough of a parenthesis, in a sort of Marshes of Glynn, he soared to heights seldom reached by anyone else."[21] In the same light mood, but meaning it nevertheless, he chided a minor poet of the day for her "obscurity and digressions" and for her use of exotic or archaic diction. He called her a "connoisseur of words" and her poems a "linguistic museum."[22]

Aldrich himself had at one time been a connoisseur of words, but he had heeded the friendly criticism of Dr. Holmes, who had warned him of his fault. Aldrich learned the value of simplicity. "Fortunate was Marcus Aurelius Antoninus," Aldrich commented, "who in early youth was taught 'to abstain from rhetoric, and poetry, and fine writing'—especially the fine writing. Simplicity is art's last word."[23] He admired the structure of Herrick's verse, "simple to the verge of innocence."[24]

Aldrich's verse could also be "simple to the verge of innocence." His short imagist poem, "After the Rain," in which he records a common experience in three sharply drawn images is but one example among many:

> The rain has ceased, and in my room
> The sunshine pours an airy flood;
> And on the church's dizzy vane
> The ancient Cross is bathed in blood.
>
> From out the dripping ivy-leaves,
> Antiquely carven, gray and high,
> A dormer, facing westward, looks
> Upon the village like an eye.
>
> And now it glimmers in the sun,
> A square of gold, a disk, a speck:
> And in the belfry sits a Dove
> With purple ripples on her neck.[25]

Aldrich's respect for tradition kept him from appreciating the Romantic cult of the original. He felt that originality, in itself, was no virtue. "There is always a small coterie of highly intellectual men and women," he noted, "eager to give welcome to whatever is eccentric, obscure or chaotic. Worshippers at the shrine of the Unpopular, they tingle with a sense of tolerant superiority when they say: 'Of course this is not the kind of thing *you* would like.' "[26]

"The greatest poets," he thought, "have, with rare exceptions, been the most indebted to their predecessors or of their contemporaries. It has been wittily remarked that only mediocrity is ever wholly original. Impressionability is one of the conditions of the creative faculty: the sensitive mind is the only mind that invents. What the poet reads, sees, and feels, goes into his blood. . . . The color of his thought instinctively blends itself with the color of its affinities. A writer's style, if it have distinction, is the outcome of a hundred styles."[27]

Walt Whitman, in Aldrich's opinion, was not one of the "rare exceptions." Aldrich failed to appreciate Whitman's genius because he felt that Whitman had ignored the traditions and conventions of English poetry, that his manner was a "hollow affectation." Admitting that Whitman would "outlast the majority of his contemporaries," Aldrich felt that in the future Whitman would live only in "a glass case or a quart of spirits in an anatomical museum." Whitman's unconventional verse which is "neither prose nor verse, and certainly it is not an improvement on either," divorced him from the majority of readers. He had "a glorious line now and then, and a striking bit of color here and there"; but "where he is fine, he is fine in precisely the way of the conventional poets."[28]

Aldrich summed up his views on originality in the following quatrain:

No bird has ever uttered note
That was not in some first bird's throat;
Since Eden's freshness and man's fall
No rose has been original.

III *Critical Theories of Fiction*

Aldrich also had carefully thought-out critical theories of fiction. Although he was unable to construct a fine plot himself, he had great respect for those whose sense of form was greater than his own. In an essay, "Plot and Character," Aldrich explores the plot-character argument and comes to the conclusion that "plot approaches nearer to being character than character does to being plot" because plot necessitates action and a man cannot act without "revealing something of his character, his way of looking at things, his moral and his mental pose." In fact, Aldrich's point of view is very close to Howells' theory of Realism. Aldrich, like Howells, finally came to object to the "intrusive author" who speaks to the reader directly, thus destroying the illusion of reality that the author is trying to create. "What a hero of fiction *does*," Aldrich thought, "paints him better than what he *says* and vastly better than anything his creator may say of him." Thus there must always be a story to tell and "a story involves beginning, middle, and end—in short, a framework of some description."[29] In poetry, also, form is most important: "Be the motive grave or gay, it is given that faultlessness of form which distinguishes everything in literature that has survived its own period."[30]

IV   *Aldrich's Theories on Form and Subject*

Aldrich was at his best when he restricted his scope. He mastered the art of the short story, but he was unable to cope with the demands of the novel. He wrote his short stories by formula: starting with the last paragraph first, he then worked "directly up to that, avoiding all digressions and side issues." He complained that his characters talked too much. "They *will* talk, and I have to let them," he wrote, "but when the story is finished, I go over the dialogue and strike out four fifths of the long speeches."[31]

In poetry, as in fiction, Aldrich excelled in the shorter form: undoubtedly he should be remembered for his lyrics, sonnets, and quatrains rather than for his long narrative poetry. He had a rare understanding of the quatrain especially. "It is a suprisingly difficult form of poem," he wrote. "The difficulty of its construction is all out of proportion to its brevity. A perfect quatrain is almost as rare as a perfect sonnet. . . . The quatrain has laws as imperious as those of the sonnet, and not to be broken with impunity. Four lines do not necessarily constitute a quatrain proper any more than fourteen lines necessarily constitute a sonnet. If your little stanza ends with a snap, it becomes an *epigram* and ceases to be a poem. The idea or thought expressed must be so fully expressed as to leave no material for a second stanza. The theme that can be exhausted in the space of four lines is not easy to light on."[32] Aldrich claimed to have written forty or fifty quatrains but not more than five or six of them satisfied him. He never mentioned which five or six they were, but the following verses are typical of the ones he included in the definitive edition of his poetry.

COQUETTE

Or light or dark, or short or tall,
She sets a spring to snare them all;
All's one to her—above her fan
She'd make sweet eyes at Caliban.

ON HER BLUSHING

Now the red wins upon her cheek;
Now white with crimson closes
In desperate struggle—so to speak;
A War of Roses.

And the following are typical of his more serious vein.

HUMAN IGNORANCE

What mortal knows
Whence comes the tint and odor of the rose?
What probing deep
Has ever solved the mystery of sleep?

PROBLEM

So closely knit are mind and brains,
Such web and woof are soul and clay,
How is it, being rent in twain,
One part shall live, and one decay.

The sonnet, with its rigid restrictions and limited scope, was also one of Aldrich's favorite forms. He had some rather unconventional opinions about the sonnet form, much preferring the Petrarchan form "with its interwoven rhyme, its capacity for expressing subtle music," to the English form with the couplet at the end which "brings the reader up with a jerk."[33] Thus to Aldrich, not Shakespeare but Milton, Wordsworth, and Keats represent the highest development of the English sonnet.

Aldrich is also Classic in spirit in his reluctance to use purely personal emotion and experience as subjects for literature. He was extremely reticent about exposing his own personal life, and he also respected others' privacy; he even regretted that Browning's personal letters had been published. Commenting on the Browning letters, Aldrich reportedly said, "a man—even the greatest—can not stand being photographed in his pajamas," and he thanked heaven we are spared Shakespeare's letters to Anne Hathaway.[34] As editor of *The Atlantic Monthly* he wrote to an unknown contributor praising the structure and craftsmanship of her sonnet, but he warned her of the danger of using "purely personal emotions" in public poetry. "Why should we print in a magazine," he asked, "those intimate revelations which he wouldn't dream of confiding to the bosom of an utter stranger at an evening party? In what respect does the stranger differ from the public which we are so ready to take into our inmost confidence?"[35]

Although Aldrich would not deny the Romantic's emphasis on inspiration, he found himself agreeing far more with Alexander Pope's dictum: "True ease in writing comes from art, not chance / as thou move easiest who have learned to dance." Poets then, thought Aldrich, can be made as well as born, and in "Proem," one of the few poems he wrote solely on the poetic craft, he explains how his poems were made:

I

You ask us if by rule or no
Our many-colored songs are wrought:

Upon the cunning loom of thought
We weave our fancies, so and so.

II

The busy shuttle comes and goes
Across the rhymes, and deftly weaves
A tissue out of autumn leaves,
With here a thistle, there a rose.

III

With art and patience thus is made
The poet's perfect Cloth of Gold:
When woven so, nor moth nor mould
Nor time can make its colors fade.[36]

Art and patience, then, are both vitally necessary. But Aldrich also realized the danger involved when Art for Art is carried to an extreme. Technique is always important, but it should not become an end in itself. In praising Dobson's poems, he declared that Dobson had the "grace of Suckling and the finish of Herrick" and that he was "easily the master of both in metrical art." But he also noted that "Mr. Dobson's triolets, rondels, rondeaus, and other imitations of French verse are examples of his exceeding great skill; but even the lowest slope of Parnassus is too good a site for a gymnasium." Although he admired Dobson's poetry, he regretted that "Dobson's facility sometimes [lured] him into being merely artificial."[37]

Aldrich summarized his critical theory in the poem "Art."

"Let art be all in all," one time I said,
And straightway stirred the hypercritic gall.
I said not, "Let technique be all in all,"
But art—a wider meaning. Worthless, dead—
The shell without its pearl, the corpse of things—
Mere words are, till the spirit lend them wings.
The poet who wakes no soul within his lute
Falls short of art: 'twere better he were mute.

The workmanship wherewith the gold is wrought
Adds yet a richness to the richest gold;
Who lacks the art to shape his thought, I hold,
Were little poorer if he lacked the thought.
The statue's slumber were unbroken still
In the dull marble, had the hand no skill.
Disparage not the magic touch that gives
The formless thought the grace whereby it lives![38]

V *A Nineteenth-Century Neo-Humanist*

It cannot be said that Aldrich was Classical in the sense that he was a Classical scholar, nor did he consciously follow Greek and Latin forms; but he was Classical in the manner of Paul Elmer More, one of the leading neo-Humanists. In fact, he anticipates what Van Wyck Brooks has called the Classical reaction—neo-Humanism—in American criticism. The fact that Aldrich has not been recognized as a forerunner of the neo-Humanists is due primarily to his continued reluctance to write formal literary criticism. But his similarity to them is there nonetheless.

Aldrich shared the neo-Humanists' disgust for Realism and Naturalism, especially as evidenced in poetry. Complaining in a letter to F. D. Sherman on the state of poetry, he wrote: "It is plain that the poetry in demand today must be strong, and picturesque and slangish with a dash of obscenity. Henceforth, the muse shall wear a cabbage and not a rose on her bosom. . . ."[39] And although he admired Kipling's short stories, he despised his verse primarily because he hated all dialect poetry. His enormous respect for the English language made him intolerant of the lack of respect certain so-called poets—radicals and local colorists—seemed to have for it. He had a plan to satirize the popular taste in poetry by putting the "Eve of St. Agnes" into Kiplingese, but he never rewrote more than the following lines:

St. Hagnes Heve! 'ow bloomin' chill it was!
The Howl, for all his hulster, was a-cold.
The 'are limped tremblin' through the blarsted grass,
Etc. etc.

"I think it might make Keats popular again," he wrote, "—poor Keats, who didn't know any better than to write pure English."[40]

Aldrich also shared the neo-Humanists' distrust of reform and reformers. "I have come to the conclusion," he wrote to his old friend, William Winter, "that more than half the mischief done in this world is done with the best intentions. Look at the shortsighted, intolerant prohibitionists, the howling women suffragettes and the raving maniacs who are banging their heads against both sides of the fence. They all mean well—confound them!"[41]

His belief that poets should avoid topical subjects is also in the neo-Humanist vein. His aloofness, he admitted, was due in part to a lack of quick sympathies with contemporary experience. Even though he confessed to a few poems of topical interest such as "Elmwood," "Wendell Phillips," "Unguarded Gates," and the "Shaw Memorial Ode," these poems are not typical Aldrich. "A good poem on some passing event," he wrote, "is certain of instant success; but when the event is passed, few things are more certain of oblivion." He believed that a poem should express beauty, a loveliness that can be appreciated in any age. This loveliness or beauty "will outlive nine tenths of the noisy verse of our stress and storm period." The poet who "never dreamed of having a Mission" will live long after "all the shrill didactic singers" have been left "high and dry 'on the sands of time.' "[42]

Aldrich's respect for the value of Classical standards, for tradition, his condemnation of contemporary literature, his lack of interest in science, his hatred for vulgarity and excess are also in the neo-Humanist vein. Although he did not share

Paul Elmer More's deep sense of evil in the world, at least Aldrich did not value it as a subject for poetry. He was like More in other ways also; but, unlike most professional writers, because he no longer needed to write for money during the latter part of his life, he wrote but little literary criticism. No doubt Aldrich would have been an excellent critic, a vanguard of the much-needed restraining voice that was not heard effectively until the neo-Humanists spoke, decades later.

CHAPTER 6

Reputation

ALDRICH, toward the end of his life, sadly predicted the change in literary tastes that he astutely sensed—a change that plunged him from one of the leading poets and writers of his era to a now almost-forgotten minor figure who is remembered, if at all, for a nostalgic glimpse into New England boyhood in *The Story of a Bad Boy* and for one short story still anthologized, "Marjorie Daw." He had been a phenomenal success—as poet, novelist, editor—but because he was sensitive to and aware of literary trends, he realized that twentieth-century readers would not concern themselves with his creative works. In a letter to his friend Frank Dempster Sherman, Aldrich admits that his kind of poetry was "steadily going out of fashion, perhaps never to come into fashion again."[1] And he regretted the rise of the new school of poets that were to become popular in the early decades of the twentieth century. No doubt he had in mind the poetry of Stephen Crane, Edwin Arlington Robinson, and Vachel Lindsay, the poets who won critical recognition and some popularity in the early twentieth century while Aldrich, with his skilled craftsmanship and polished form, was ignored and then forgotten.

How and why did this happen? His instant youthful success; his continuing literary growth; his rise to the pinnacle of the intellectual, literary world; and then, after his death, his almost immediate oblivion do, of course, parallel the literary transition—in form, subject matter, and philosophical outlook—that took place from the nineteenth century to the twentieth. And Aldrich was a man who belonged to the nineteenth century. It was the nineteenth century that lionized him, the twentieth century that forgot him.

I Youthful Success

Aldrich, at the age of nineteen, became a national celebrity. His early success as a poet was fantastic because his sentimental Muse, which then had the upper hand, readily appealed to the damp tastes of the emotional 1850's. Thus, when he published "Babie Bell" in a commercial publication, *The Journal of Commerce,* "it swept through the country like a piece of news,"[2] and Aldrich's literary career started with a magnificent flourish. Not only did he win popular acclaim, but he also earned the praise of one of the leading literary figures of New York, Fitz-Greene Halleck, who asserted that Aldrich was "much more promising" than most of his contemporaries and who hoped that he would be persuaded to work on.[3] Halleck did even more by asserting in *Putnam's Monthly* that "there was not a line in 'Babie Bell' that he could alter."[4] Coming from a highly respected figure such as Fitz-Greene Halleck was at the time, this was high praise indeed for an aspiring poet of nineteen. "Babie Bell" also had the approval of Nathaniel P. Willis, another important writer and editor of the 1850's, who reprinted it in his *Home Journal.*

A contemporary evaluation of Aldrich's other adolescent works by an anonymous reviewer hailed him as the youngest and most promising of our poets, and praised "Babie Bell" for its touching pathos, its exquisite imagery, and its effective climax. The reviewer, who even had pleasant things to say of *Daisy's Necklace,* praised it for its dainty conceits, exuberant fancies, and, again, exquisite imagery. He concluded that a sensuousness of rare grace pervades all that Aldrich writes and makes him characteristically a poet of the Beautiful. Of course this kind of newspaper notice cannot be taken seriously as literary criticism, but it was encouraging to Aldrich who had recently given up the mercantile security of his uncle's countinghouse for the precarious life of a professional literary man.

Although he was recognized as a promising poet of national reputation before he was twenty, Aldrich was not content to stagnate. In spite of heavy duties as sub-editor of the *Home Journal*, he continued to write verses, to revise them, and to reject them. He established from the very beginning his habit of carefully editing his own work. In 1856, setting his goals high, he wrote to Fields, of the famed Boston publishing company of Ticknor & Fields, offering his poems to Fields for publication: "From some 50 poems which I have written since the (cow) [sic] 'Bells' was published, I have selected 25 which I think will pass critical muster."[5] Aldrich, however, was not quite ready for the sanction of literary Boston, for Fields rejected this first attempt.

Aldrich did not have long to wait, though, for in 1858 he published *The Course of True Love Never Did Run Smooth*, an Arabian love story told in Tennysonian verse, which even won the praise of the dean of the New England poets, Henry Wadsworth Longfellow. "The poem," the elder poet wrote, "is very charming, full of color and perfume as a rose. I congratulate you on your success."[6] Longfellow also invited Aldrich to visit him in Boston, a prized invitation; and he assured him of continued interest in the young poet's career. Such sincere praise from the most-loved poet of the day not only was encouraging in itself but was also indicative that Aldrich was already getting the attention of the New England literary giants.

Continuing his practice of carefully editing his work and of rejecting with impeccable taste those poems he considered inferior, Aldrich published two volumes of poetry, *The Ballad* of *Babie Bell and Other Poems* (1859) and *Pampinea and Other Poems* (1861). His work showed steady improvement. The first volume was lauded by William Dean Howells, the young literary critic of the *Saturday Press,* a Bohemian journal more often given to satire than to praise. Howells' comments show that he recognized and appreciated some of Aldrich's essential characteristics that the young poet was to refine continuously as he matured. Howells especially commented on the poem "Nameless Pain" which, he wrote, "is the worthiest proof that Mr. Aldrich is a poet. . . . All hearts . . . feel sometimes the Nameless Pain, only different in degree. How it thrills and trembles in the heart of the poet he has—described? No. Expressed? No. We do not, even the greatest-tongued of us, describe or express intense sensation. The best that any can do is to let the soul be seen for an instant with the secret lightening of feeling playing through it, and illuming it. . . ."[7] Of course Howells did not have the stature as a critic in 1858 that he was later to achieve, but the *Saturday Press* had a respectable reputation. Being praised in its pages was almost as coveted as being praised in the all-important *Atlantic Monthly.*

The *Atlantic Monthly* under the editorship of James Russell Lowell was rapidly becoming recognized as the undisputed, leading literary magazine of the day. Emerson, Longfellow, Harriet Beecher Stowe, and, in fact, all of the leading figures of New England were among the regular contributors. Frank Luther Mott, the eminent historian of American publications, pointed out that "*The Atlantic* may be said to have enjoyed a perpetual state of literary grace, so that for a large section of the American public, whatever the *Atlantic* printed was literature."[8]

Thus, when Aldrich received the following letter from Lowell, it meant that his work had been recognized by the literary élite of America. "My dear Sir," Lowell wrote, "I welcome you heartily to the *Atlantic.* When I receive so fine a poem as 'Pythagoras,' I don't think the check of Messrs. Ticknor & Fields pays for it. I must add some thanks and appreciation. I have put it down for June."[9] In the same year of 1860, Aldrich sold two more poems—"The Song of Fatima" and "The Robin"—to the *Atlantic;* and, from then on, he became a regular contributor which meant that his literary reputation was, if not secure, at least firmly grounded.

Although Fields had declined to accept Aldrich's poems, Rudd and Carleton, a New York publishing firm, did print *Pampinea and Other Poems* in 1861. Again Longfellow was generous in his praise, especially of the lyric "Piscataqua," named for the river that was so important to Aldrich's New England youth. Longfellow thought that the poem lived and moved and had "its being in the realm of Imagination, 'clothing the palpable and familiar with golden exhalations of the dawn.'" He believed, too, that the river would "always be more beautiful for that song!"[10] Though Aldrich later regretted publishing *Pampinea and Other Poems* and destroyed every copy he could acquire, the volume contained several individual poems that he considered good enough to be included in subsequent editions.

The 1863 edition of his poetry entitled *Poems* brought him to the attention of Oliver Wendell Holmes, who wrote him a letter of kind criticism and genuine praise. The fact that the letter was long and obviously sincere indicated that Holmes thought that Aldrich was a promising poet who merely needed to learn restraint to mature.

II *The Mark of Fame: Blue and Gold*

The praise of Holmes and Longfellow, combined with the approval of Lowell who accepted Aldrich's poems for the *Atlantic,* probably finally persuaded Fields to publish a collection of Aldrich's poetry in the handsome and prestige-laden "Blue and Gold Series." Only the most distinguished contemporary poets were fortunate enough to appear under that honored label, for Ticknor and Fields reserved publication for a very select group: poets whom Ticknor and Fields considered to have reached their literary maturity and now deserved to be ranked with Lowell, Holmes, Whittier, and Longfellow. There was no American Academy of Arts and Letters to recognize officially any distinguished literary achievement, but being published in the Ticknor and Fields' "Blue and Gold Series" amounted to the same thing: it was unquestionably the highest honor a poet could earn in America in the 1860's. When Aldrich's volume came out in 1865 under the title of *The Poems of Thomas Bailey Aldrich,* it meant that his reputation as a poet was firmly established. The following year he was recognized abroad in the *Athenaeum* where he was compared with Longfellow and described as "an addition to that small band of American poets that is so slowly reinforced."[11]

Aldrich did not rest on his laurels; he continued to polish his style and to reject inferior poems. *Cloth of Gold and Other Poems* (1874), *Flower and Thorn* (1877), *Friar Jerome's Beautiful Book, and Other Poems* (1881), and *XXXVI Lyrics and XII Sonnets* (1881) showed steady improvement. In 1897 he was honored by having a definitive collection of his poetic works published by Houghton, Mifflin in the "Household Series." The Household Edition of Aldrich's poetry contains but a fraction of his published poems, but even then he was still not satisfied with his own rigid selections.

He wanted to publish an even smaller collection of his poems that would represent his highest achievement. This he did in 1906 for the Riverside Press in *A Book of Songs and Sonnets Selected From the Poems of Thomas Bailey Aldrich.* It was this volume that won the warm praise of the astute Paul Elmer More who recognized Aldrich's Classical origins and who claimed that readers of the future would "hold in memory the falling petals of the *Songs and Sonnets* long after [they have] forgotten more ambitious things."¹² And the erudite critic and historian of American letters, Fred Lewis Pattee, shared More's enthusiasm for the later lyrics. Pattee wrote: "He will go down as the most finished poet that America has yet produced . . . the maker of trifles that were miracles of art, and finally as the belated singer who awoke in his later years to message and vision and produced with his mastered art a handful of perfect lyrics that rank with the strongest that America has given to song."¹³ This is strong praise from a critic who tended to prefer the Realists. Thus during his lifetime and a decade or so after his death in 1907, Aldrich's reputation as an important American poet seemed secure.

III   *Fame as Fiction Writer*

But his fame as a writer of fiction was even more widely acclaimed. His early attempts at fiction, with the exception of "Père Antoine's Date-Palm," drew little attention, but all that was changed radically when in 1870 he published in book form *The Story of a Bad Boy*. It had appeared previously as a serial in the *Atlantic Monthly* in 1869 and had considerably brightened the pages of that stately journal. In March of that year William Dean Howells wrote to Aldrich: "I read your Bad Boy's Fourth of July . . . and was made to laugh beyond reason by turns."¹⁴ And, when the novel appeared in book form and Howells had time to give it real critical attention, he was still warm in his appreciation. While he objected mildly to the intrusive author and felt that the Irish characters were not so well done, he recognized the novelty of the work and was enthusiastic about the realistic portraits of the New England characters—especially the Captain, Miss Abigail, and Binny Wallace—and praised the incident of Binny Wallace's dramatic but realistic death. A favorable review in the *Atlantic Monthly* was almost a guarantee for the success of a novel, and *The Story of a Bad Boy* nearly sold enough copies to make it a best seller.

The Story of a Bad Boy was not only a commercial success in America, but had a wide European sale and contributed considerably to Aldrich's increasing international fame. There was an English edition in 1870, and it was translated into Dutch and German in 1875. Years later Aldrich recalled that the book was "enormously successful" and—perhaps a sure sign of success—two Sunday School libraries refused to buy it.[15] It is still mentioned favorably in most American literary histories and in histories of the novel for its realistic portrayal of a boy, for its "bright description and amusing episodes," and for its "vivid narrative of credible people in an authentic setting."[16] But, since it is now out of print, few readers have the chance to judge for themselves.

No single volume contributed more to Aldrich's national and international fame than the 1873 collection of short stories, *Marjorie Daw and Other People*. The title story shows Aldrich's brilliant skill as an artificer; and since—as Howells noticed—the surprise ending was a new device in that day, the collection was extremely popular both at home and abroad. Howells felt that Aldrich had almost created a new species of fiction "in which character and incident constantly verge with us toward the brink of a quite precipitous surprise, without being for a moment less delightful as character and incident, and without being less so even when we look up at them from the gulf into which they have plunged us."[17]

Howells also felt that Marjorie Daw "lives" in spite of the author's surprise ending (she is only an imagined character), and Eunice Comstock, who wrote a poem on "Marjorie Daw" for the *Atlantic Monthly*, thought so too. Her closing stanzas echo Howell's sentiments:

> And summer moons must ever softly touch
> Each golden coil upon that head;

> For we, her lovers, will not yield so much
> As one pale, silken, shining thread.
> For having once bestowed this precious gift,
> The hand that gave may not withdraw,
> So long as light shall change and shadows shift,
> So long shall live rare Marjorie Daw.[18]

It was "Marjorie Daw" even more than *The Story of a Bad Boy* that earned Aldrich his international reputation as a humorist. The French particularly appreciated it, and in 1873 the story appeared in *Revue des Deux Mondes.* Two years later it appeared in book form in Paris, along with *Prudence Palfrey,* "Mademoiselle Olympe Zabriski" and "Père Antoine's Date-Palm." It was also printed in Rome in 1900.

Aldrich's novels, *Prudence Palfrey, The Queen of Sheba,* and *The Stillwater Tragedy,* did little to augment his ultimate reputation; but they were good enough to arouse the interest of his contemporary American and European readers. *Prudence Palfrey* was praised by Howells in the *Atlantic Monthly* and by Oliver Wendell Holmes in a long letter to Aldrich. In spite of its absurd plot, Aldrich's brilliant style saved it from being an inferior work. It was pirated by an English magazine, and it was translated into Dutch, French, and twice into German, once in 1874 and again in 1877. Even twentieth-century critics have good things to say of it. Admitting that the plot is absurd, Alexander Cowie nevertheless thinks that Aldrich caught "the accent of life, the murmur of history in the making, the gradual incorporation of life into philosophy, the formation of regional character."[19]

The Queen of Sheba was also warmly praised and internationally successful: it was translated into French, German, and Spanish. His last novel, *The Stillwater Tragedy,* was not so successful; and even his close friend Howells took him to task for breaking the illusion he was trying to create by speaking in his own first person.[20] Since Aldrich seemed unable to show improvement in plot construction, he was wise in abandoning the novel form after *The Stillwater Tragedy*. He did publish two more volumes of short stories, *Two Bites at a Cherry, with Other Tales* in 1894 and *A Sea Turn and Other Matters* in 1902; these are among his best works of fiction.

IV *Among the Most Prominent*

Thus during his lifetime, Aldrich had a faithful reading public, and he had earned the reputation of being one of America's foremost men of letters. In 1884 the editors of *The Critic*, a New York literary magazine, conducted a poll of their readers who were asked to name forty American male authors most worthy to be included in a possible American academy. The results were tabulated in the order of the number of votes. Oliver Wendell Holmes, James Russell Lowell, and John Greenleaf Whittier were the first three; Aldrich, who was seventh, was outranked by George Bancroft, William Dean Howells, and George William Curtis. But Aldrich outranked Bret Harte, George W. Cable, Henry James, Mark Twain, Walt Whitman, and John Burroughs.

The editors of *The Harvard Crimson*, at Harvard University, took a similar vote. The Harvard list is even more astounding. George William Curtis led the list and Aldrich was second, outranking Holmes, who was fifth; Lowell, who was sixth; and Henry James and Whittier, who were tenth and eleventh. Howells was fourteenth, and Mark Twain was a mere twentieth.

In 1896, Harvard University, where Aldrich had hoped to study but could not because of his father's death, awarded him an honorary degree. He wrote to his friend G. E. Woodbury that he had been reading his Harvard diploma. "You will please to understand," he humorously wrote, "that I am *virum Litteris deditum, scriptorem elegantem, narratorem facetum, poetam ingenii ubertate et varium et multiplicem,* and try to treat me with some little respect."[21] Although Aldrich wrote in jest, he was justifiably proud of the respect shown to him by the most distinguished university of his time, and by the one he had wanted to attend more than any other.

In 1899 John K. Bangs, the editor of *Literature*, polled his readers to select ten authors to be charter members of an American Academy. In the first counting, Howells was first, Twain third, and Aldrich fourth. A month later Howells was still first, but Twain had crept up to second and Aldrich retained his position in fourth place. The final results were tabulated as follows:

W. D. Howells	T. B. Aldrich
John Fiske	Frank R. Stockton
Mark Twain	Henry James
S. Weir Mitchell	John Burroughs
Bret Harte	Edmund C. Stedman[22]

When the National Academy of Arts and Letters was actually founded in 1904, Aldrich was among the first fifteen chosen for membership. During his lifetime Aldrich enjoyed the respect of his fellow authors and of a wide and faithful American and European public. After his death in 1907, there was the expected spate of flattering obituaries in all of the leading literary magazines. Ferris Greenslet's admirable biography appeared the following year, and it occasioned Paul Elmer More's appreciative essay on Aldrich's verse.

V *Aldrich's Eclipse*

Then followed a long period of silence. What Aldrich had expected had actually occurred: his poetry had gone out of fashion. He had foreseen the rise of Realism and Naturalism, but he had refused to join any literary bandwagon. His artistic integrity would not permit him to change his subject matter or his style merely to satisfy current taste. The commitment of the poet as he envisioned it is best expressed in the following near-perfect sonnet:

Enamored architect of airy rhyme,
Build as thou wilt, heed not what each man says:
Good souls, but innocent of dreamers' ways,
Will come, and marvel why thou wastest time;
Others, beholding how thy turrets climb
'Twixt theirs and heaven, will hate thee all thy days;
But most beware of those who come to praise.
O Wondersmith, O worker in sublime
And heaven-sent dreams, let art be all in all;
Build as thou wilt, unspoiled by praise or blame,
Build as thou wilt, and as thy light is given;
Then, if at last the airy structure fall,
Dissolve, and vanish—take thyself no shame.
They fail, and they alone, who have not striven.[23]

But the twentieth century had little use for airy structures, heaven-sent dreams, or art as "all in all." Whitman's "barbaric yawp" was finally getting a hearing, and the more vigorous verse of Vachel Lindsay, Edwin Arlington Robinson, and Edwin Markham better suited the taste of the age. And Aldrich's conservative attitude, evidenced not only in his political and social thinking but in his critical theories of poetry as well, was also out of step with the new era. For him, form and conventions had been permanently established; he therefore objected to Whitman's verse form which he could not consider verse at all and to Emily Dickinson's rhymes and rhythmical variations. But it was, of course, Whitman and Emily Dickinson who appealed to the twentieth century, not Aldrich. The major poets of the first half of our century were all experimenters in verse form. We have only to recall the work of Ezra Pound, T. S. Eliot, William Carlos Williams, Vachel Lindsay, Carl Sandburg, and E. E. Cummings to understand the daring spirit of what has been called "the twentieth-century renaissance." The tremendous poetic activity of the nineteenth century both in England and

America nearly exhausted the conventional verse patterns, or so it seemed to twentieth-century poets. Thus the nineteenth-century poets who experimented—Walt Whitman and Emily Dickinson in America and Gerard Manley Hopkins in England—became popular, while the traditional poets like Lowell, Longfellow, Tennyson, and Aldrich were ignored.

Along with the abrupt change of poetical taste, the rise of Naturalism, which was deeply rooted in nineteenth-century pessimism and skepticism, contributed to Aldrich's total eclipse. The brooding, probing poetry of Edwin Arlington Robinson and the questioning, skeptical writing of Henry Adams appealed to an epoch that had experienced the onslaught of science on accepted religious beliefs—that had been left, in the words of Matthew Arnold, "between two worlds, one dead, the other powerless to be born." Aldrich, who gently spoofed the science of his era and who deliberately avoided morbidity and uncertainty in his poetry, had little to say to a generation that finally recognized *The Waste Land* as one of the most significant poems of the century.

It is not fair to Aldrich to say that he was not at all moved by the spiritual crisis of his time. He did write the pessimistic poem, "The Shipman's Tale," in the mood of Stephen Crane. But that mood is not characteristically Aldrich. He later regretted that he had written in that negative vein because he believed that the function of poetry was to encourage humanity, not to discourage it. As we have already noted, his attitude was that, if a poet does not have some message of hope or consolation concerning spiritual matters, he had better avoid such subjects or remain silent. But this attitude is alien to the climate of opinion of the twentieth century; Aldrich's airy, heaven-sent dreams seems too optimistic, shallow and superficial to readers accustomed to the gloomy strength of Robinson, Masters, or Robinson Jeffers.

The early twentieth century was not only interested in man's spiritual wasteland, but was vitally concerned with immediate, pressing social problems. Jack London, Upton Sinclair, Lincoln Steffens, Edgar Lee Masters, Sherwood Anderson, and later Theodore Dreiser, John Steinbeck, and James Farrell examined the social scene and were appalled by the poverty, ignorance, and corruption they discovered in American contemporary life. Again, this interest in immediate problems was almost totally foreign to Aldrich who did not consider society's ugliness as a suitable subject for lasting poetry. On one of the rare occasions when he was sufficiently moved to write about a contemporary problem, he composed "Unguarded Gates," a poem about America's immigration policy. This was the era of the huge immigrations from Eastern and Southern Europe, and the poem's anti-immigrant sentiments and ultraconservative spirit did not endear its author to the more liberal-minded writers and readers of the twentieth century. These lines would certainly not have been selected for the permanent inscription on the Statue of Liberty:

> . . . Wide open and unguarded stand our gates,
> And through them passes a motley throng—
> Men from the Volga and the Tartar steppes,
> Featureless figures of the Hoang-Ho,
> Malayan, Scythian, Teuton, Kelt, and Slav,
> Flying the Old World's poverty and scorn;
> These bringing with them unknown gods and rites,
> These, tiger passions, here to stretch their claws.
> In street and alley what strange tongues are loud,
> Accents of menace alien to our air,
> Voices that once the Tower of Babel knew!
>
> O Liberty, white Goddess! is it well
> To leave the gates unguarded?[24]

And Aldrich's last novel, *The Stillwater Tragedy*, while not the anti-labor novel as it has been called, is in opposition to the general strike; and Aldrich's pro-management sentiments are obvious in spite of his sincere efforts to be impartial. Had Aldrich been able to continue in the realistic mood of *The*

Stillwater Tragedy, he would have appealed more to later generations; but he abandoned the novel form and perhaps wisely, since his acknowledged conservative sentiments would not have been appreciated by an age that took social problems as literary subjects seriously. Unlike William Dean Howells, whose social thinking became more liberal as he grew older, Aldrich became more conservative. He was not only opposed to revolution; he was opposed to change, even objecting to the introduction of horsecars on Charles Street in Boston. His extremely conservative, almost reactionary attitude alienated him from the liberal spirit that dominated the twentieth century.

Nor do Aldrich's short stories, with a few exceptions, deal with social problems. His one notable attempt, "Shaw's Folly," only serves to prove that he was incapable of profound social criticism. Neither does his short fiction deal with profound psychological or philosophical themes. Unlike Melville, Hawthorne, Mark Twain, and Stephen Crane, Aldrich does not delve into the potential for evil in the hearts of man. The theme of the effect of intellectual pride on human character, so intriguing to Hawthorne, and the mysteries of human existence and of man's tragic position that plagued Melville, are foreign to Aldrich. And the rage that Stephen Crane felt at the bigotry and petty cruelty of the outwardly respectable American middle class did not move Aldrich. Aldrich did know that tragedy could occur in daily life, but his treatment of it was calmly Realistic, as in "For Bravery on the Field of Battle," rather than Naturalistic, as in Crane's "The Monster." In Aldrich's story, tragedy occurs through thoughtless neglect of well-meaning people rather than through active prejudice. The sterner, more unforgiving treatment of American life as depicted by Crane is more in the mood of the twentieth century than Aldrich's; his stories seem tame to contemporary readers who are steeped in the violence of Hemingway, the decadence of Faulkner, and the severe, bit-ing social criticism of Farrell and O'Hara. Thus, despite Aldrich's skillfully constructed plots, his carefully prepared surprise endings, and his never-failing wit, his fiction does not have the bold impact nor the social seriousness that our time demands. Until our literary taste changes and makes it possible for us again to appreciate literary craftmanship for its own sake, Aldrich's fiction and his poetry will remain in oblivion.

VI *Posthumous Criticism*

The most devastating influence contributing to the decline of Aldrich's literary reputation was the widespread post-World War I reaction to nineteenth-century Victorianism and gentility. Under the leadership of H. L. Mencken and others, middle-class respectability, which was thought to be a legacy from both nineteenth-century gentility and New England Puritanism, was held up to ridicule. Mencken's bombastic and thoroughly inaccurate essay, "Puritanism, A Literary Force," was taken with high seriousness by the "liberated" intellects of the 1920's. It was a wholesale condemnation of Cooper, Irving, Longfellow, Emerson, and even Poe. Whittier and Lowell were "frank second raters"; and the popularity of the New England literary figures, Mencken thought, was "a sufficient indication of the crudeness of the current taste and the mean position assigned to the art of letters."[25]

Aldrich received his share of the abuse in an article in the *American Mercury* by C. Hartly Grattan who declared Aldrich "never had anything to say," "never looked at life directly," and wrote "escape poetry of the most vapid sort." Aldrich's much-admired poem, "Spring in New England," was, according to Grattan, "word dropping of a pious sentimentality for the war victims buried in the far away South." Even *The Story of a Bad Boy* was condemned by Grattan because in his opinion it did not compare to *Huckleberry Finn*.[26] Grattan did note Aldrich's similarity to the seventeenth-century Herrick, but he compared them unfavorably. Herrick, Grattan felt, had a meaningful *carpe diem* theme and had a strong identification with the English countryside; the implication is, of course, that Aldrich did not. Even a casual reading of Aldrich's poetry makes Grattan's criticism seem at best irresponsible. Aldrich certainly made use of the *carpe diem* theme. We need but recall "I'll Not Confer with Sorrow," "An Untimely Thought," "Amontillado," and many other poems to realize Aldrich's concern with the timeless theme of transience. His use of the *carpe diem* theme, while not so pervasive as Herrick's, is nonetheless present in a significant number of poems, all demonstrating his emotional reaction to the pathos of the passing of time. And Aldrich, like Herrick, knew and loved the area of his birth. "Spring in New England," "Piscataqua River," "Seadrift," "Landscape," and numerous other regional poems testify to Aldrich's keen observation and his continuing love of the New England landscape, its river, its ocean, its forbidding coast.

Even more influential in the death of Aldrich's reputation than Grattan was Vernon Louis Parrington's dismissal of Aldrich in his provocative and highly readable *Main Currents in American Thought.* "Marjorie Daw" was "thin and artificial, too consciously written backwards from a surprise ending." *The Story of a Bad Boy* was unfavorably compared to *Huckleberry Finn;* and Aldrich, like Lowell, was dismissed as a "pseudo intellectual" and a victim of "capitalistic prejudice."[27] Parrington's enormous reputation and his imposing work dominated American literary studies for a long time, and his deprecating remarks about the New England writers did them an injustice. His criticisms of Aldrich are only true in part and are evidence of Parrington's liberal bias. We would not expect him to admire the work of Aldrich, a staunch conservative.

Aldrich also suffered from his association with Bayard Taylor, E. C. Stedman, and the other writers of the so-called "genteel tradition" of New York. Typical of this condemnation by association is Willard Thorp's paragraph on Aldrich in *American Writing in the Twentieth Century* in which he wrote that Aldrich brought gentility to Boston with him in 1861 and that he and Stoddard and Stedman were defenders of the "Ideal" in literature and had sought to preserve the "True" and the "Beautiful" from the taint of Naturalism and other foreign contaminations.[28] It is a curious notion to think of Aldrich as bringing gentility to Boston which was, of course, the center of gentility long before Aldrich arrived. And, in fairness to Aldrich, we should recall that, while he kept up his friendship with Stedman and Taylor, he had all but abandoned the sentimental Romantic gentility of his friends and had developed, as editor of the *Atlantic Monthly* and as a writer, a clearly defined and persistent Classicism.

Because Aldrich lacked the reforming spirit, would not accept Realism and Naturalism, maintained his own literary principles, and did not use literature to explore the more profound, complex problems of the human spirit, he has been neglected by twentieth-century readers—to their loss. Not all fine writing must, of necessity, be profound or philosophical; nor must it be militantly reforming. There is a place for amusing, lighthearted stories and for carefully constructed, highly polished verse that is unpretentious in its aims and that is written for pure delight. To have a permanent place in literature, every novel does not have to be a *Moby Dick* or a *Huckleberry Finn;* every poem need not be a *Leaves of Grass* or *The Waste Land*. Perhaps this statement is another way of saying there is room in American literature not only for our major talents but for our competent minor literary figures. Aldrich's fiction, particularly his short stories, can still be appreciated for their wit, humor, and skillful narration; and those who will take the trouble to read his collected poems will find they contain many verses as good or better than the poets of the New England Renaissance and all are far superior to his contemporaries of the "so-called" genteel school. Thomas Bailey Aldrich should be remembered as our outstanding minor poet.

Notes and References

Chapter One

1. Ferris Greenslet, *Thomas Bailey Aldrich* (Boston and New York, 1908), p. 160. Unless otherwise indicated, all biographical facts are from Greenslet's authorized biography.

2. Quoted in Greenslet, pp. 79-80.

3. *Ibid.*

4. Mrs. Thomas Bailey Aldrich, *Crowding Memories* (Boston and New York, 1920), p. 102.

5. Letter, Aldrich to William Winter, undated. Quoted in William Winter, *Old Friends* (New York, 1909), p. 144.

6. *Crowding Memories*, p. 102.

7. Letter, Howells to Aldrich, November 20, 1901. #2359, Widener Library.

8. Letter, Howells to Aldrich, December 8, 1901. #2360, Widener Library.

9. Quoted in Greenslet, p. 81.

10. Thomas Wentworth Higginson, *Cheerful Yesterdays* (New York, 1898).

11. M. A. DeWolfe Howe, *Memories of a Hostess* (Boston, 1922), pp. 292ff.

12. Thomas Bailey Aldrich, *The Story of a Bad Boy* in *The Works of Thomas Bailey Aldrich* (Cambridge, 1897), VII, 7. All references to Aldrich's writings will be to this edition unless otherwise indicated; hereafter referred to as *Works*.

13. Thomas Bailey Aldrich, "Farewell," in Jacob Blank, *Bibliography of American Literature* (New Haven, 1955), I, 46.

14. Greenslet, pp. 10-11.

15. Aldrich, *Works*, VII, 268.

16. Letter, Thomas Bailey Aldrich to William Dean Howells, May 12, 1902, in Mildred Howells, *Life and Letters of William Dean Howells* (New York, 1928), II, 158.

17. Aldrich, *An Old Town by the Sea, Works,* VIII, 200, 201.

18. *Ibid.,* p. 186.

19. Aldrich, *The Story of a Bad Boy,* Works, VII, 39-41. The Bailey house in Portsmouth has been restored almost exactly as

Aldrich described it and is now known as the Aldrich Memorial Museum.

20. *Ibid.*
21. *Ibid.*, pp. 40-41.
22. Howe, *op. cit.*, p. 292.
23. Greenslet, p. 14.
24. *The Story of a Bad Boy, Works*, VII, 58.
25. Howe, *op. cit.*, pp. 292ff.
26. *Old Town by the Sea, Works*, VIII, 187-89.
27. "Piscataqua River," *Works*, I, 7-8.
28. *The Story of a Bad Boy, Works*, VII, 42.
29. *An Old Town by the Sea, Works*, VIII, 19.
30. For the following descriptions of old Portsmouth houses, I have relied heavily on *An Old Town by the Sea.* For this study, Aldrich's memory of the town is more important than literal accuracy.
31. Letter from Aldrich to William Winter, quoted in Greenslet, p. 30.
32. J. C. Derby, *Fifty Years Among Authors, Books and Publishers* (New York, 1884).
33. Charles T. Congdon, *Reminiscences of a Journalist* (Boston, 1880), pp. 356ff.
34. Gilbert Donaldson, "Thomas Bailey Aldrich" *The Reader,* IX (May, 1907), 660.
35. Winter, *op. cit.* p. 146.
36. *Ibid.*, pp. 136-37.
37. Donaldson, *op. cit.*, p. 660.
38. George William Curtis, *The Potiphar Papers* (New York, 1853), *passim.*
39. Aldrich, *Out of His Head, A Romance* (New York, 1862), pp. 162-72.
40. Richard Stoddard, *Recollections Personal and Literary* (New York, 1903), p. 253.
41. *Ibid.*, p. 192.
42. *Ibid.*
43. Winter, *op. cit.*, p. 355.
44. Albert Parry, *Garrets and Pretenders* (New York, 1933), p. 9.
45. Winter, *op. cit.*, p. 40.
46. *Ibid.*, p. 64.
47. *Ibid.*, pp. 57-59.
48. *Ibid.*, p. 139.

49. *Ibid.*
50. *Ibid.*
51. Letter, Aldrich to Bayard Taylor, November 26, 1865. #6, Cornell University Library.

Chapter Two

1. Thomas Bailey Aldrich, *The Bells: A Collection of Chimes* (New York, 1855).
2. Greenslet, pp. 99-100.
3. Aldrich, *Works*, I, 52.
4. Aldrich, *The Bells*, p. 100.
5. William Winter, *Old Friends* (New York, 1909), p. 40.
6. Aldrich, *Works*, I, 30.
7. Aldrich, *Works*, I, 45.
8. Greenslet, pp. 64-65.
9. Thomas Bailey Aldrich, *The Ballad of Babie Bell and other Poems* (New York, 1858), pp. 65-66.
10. Aldrich, *Works*, I.
11. *Works*, II, 90-91.
12. *Works*, II, 159-60.
13. *Works*, II, 203.
14. *Works*, I, 142.
15. *Works*, I, 133-34.
16. *Works*, I, 55.
17. *Works*, I, 199.
18. *Works*, I, 137.
19. *Works*, I, 45.
20. *Works*, II, 200.
21. *The Ballad of Babie Bell and other Poems*, p. 55. These lines were deleted from later editions of the poem.
22. Willard Thorp, "Defenders of Ideality," in *Literary History of the United States* ed. Robert Spiller and Willard Thorp (New York, 1948).
23. *Works*, I, 202.
24. *Works*, II, 152.
25. *Works*, I, 38-39.
26. *Works*, I, 28.
27. *Works*, I, 27.
28. Hamlin Garland, *Roadside Meetings* (New York, 1930), pp. 119-20.
29. *Works*, II, 202.

30. *Works*, I, 55.
31. *Works*, I, 61.
32. *Works*, I, 65-66.
33. *Works*, II, 178.
34. *Works*, II, 88.

Chapter Three

1. Thomas Bailey Aldrich, "What Jedd Pallfry Found in the Coffin," *The Knickerbocker*, XLIX (January, 1857), 28.
2. Greenslet, pp. 84-85.
3. *Works*, III, 295.
4. Fred Lewis Pattee, *The Development of the American Short Story* (New York, 1923), p. 214.
5. Thomas Bailey Aldrich, "A Young Desperado," *Atlantic Monthly*, XX (December, 1867), 755-58.
6. William Dean Howells, "Recent Literature," *Atlantic Monthly*, XXXII (November, 1873), 625.
7. *Works*, III, 181-225.
8. *Works*, V, 280-81.
9. *Works*, V, 283.
10. *Works*, V, 286.
11. *Works*, III, 244.
12. *Ibid.*
13. *Ibid.*, p. 245.
14. *Ibid.*, p. 270.
15. M. A. DeWolfe Howe, *Memories of a Hostess* (Boston, 1922), p. 291.
16. Thomas Bailey Aldrich, *The Ponkapog Papers, A Sea Turn and Other Matters* (Boston and New York, 1903), pp. 211-62.
17. *Works*, V, 203-62.
18. Greenslet, p. 210.
19. Annie Fields, *Letters of Sarah Orne Jewett* (Boston, 1911), p. 79.
20. Thomas Bailey Aldrich, "Shaw's Folly," *A Sea Turn and Other Matters* (Boston, 1902).
21. Fields, *op. cit.*, p. 79.

Chapter Four

1. J. C. Derby, *Fifty Years Among Authors, Books and Publishers* (New York, 1884), p. 230.
2. Walter Blair, *Mark Twain and Huck Finn* (Berkeley and Los Angeles, 1960), p. 64.

3. Letter, Aldrich to Bayard Taylor, July 1, 1877. #36, Cornell University Library.

4. Letter, Aldrich to E. C. Stedman, November 18, 1878. #1492, Widener Library.

Chapter Five

1. Letter, Aldrich to William Winter, August 15, 1855, quoted in Winter, *Old Friends*, p. 361.

2. Letter, Aldrich to Stoddard, August, 1860. New York Public Library.

3. William Winter, *Old Friends* (New York, 1909), p. 361.

4. *Works*, I, 152.

5. Gilbert Donaldson, "Thomas Bailey Aldrich," *The Reader*, IX (May, 1907), 657-65.

6. *Works*, II, 93.

7. Aldrich, *Ponkapog Papers*, p. 32.

8. *Ibid.*, p. 15.

9. *Ibid.*, p. 99.

10. *Ibid.*, p. 139.

11. *Ibid.*, p. 141.

12. Greenslet, p. 143.

13. *Ibid.*, p. 146.

14. *Ibid.*, 148.

15. *Ibid,* p. 147.

16. Aldrich, *Ponkapog Papers*, p. 34-35.

17. Letter, Aldrich to F. S. Sherman, Dec. 31, 1896. Quoted in Greenslet, p. 170.

18. Letter, Aldrich to F. S. Sherman, May 29, 1892. New York Public Library.

19. Greenslet, p. 70.

20. Winter, *op. cit.*, pp. 361-62.

21. Letter, Aldrich to E. C. Stedman, Dec. 14, 1904. Widener Library.

22. Thomas Bailey Aldrich, "Four Books of Verse," *Atlantic Monthly*, LXI (March, 1888), 416-44.

23. Aldrich, *Ponkapog Papers*, p. 28.

24. *Ibid.*, p. 41.

25. *Works*, I, 36-37.

26. Aldrich, *Ponkapog Papers*, p. 31.

27. *Ibid.*, p. 142.

28. Greenslet, pp. 138-39.

29. Aldrich, *Ponkapog Papers*, pp. 62-63.

30. *Ibid.*, p. 141.
31. *Ibid.*, p. 30.
32. Greenslet, p. 226.
33. *Ibid.*, p. 213.
34. Percy F. Bicknell, "The Story of A Poet's Life," *The Dial,* XLV (October 19, 1908), 250-52.
35. Greenslet, p. 148.
36. *Works*, I, 53.
37. Thomas Bailey Aldrich, "Dobson's Proverbs," *Atlantic Monthly*, XLIII (September, 1879), 775.
38. *Works*, II, 170.
39. Letter, Aldrich to F. S. Sherman, December 31, 1896. New York Public Library.
40. Greenslet, p. 207.
41. Winter, *op. cit.*, p. 367.
42. Greenslet, p. 200-1.

Chapter Six

1. Letter, Aldrich to Frank S. Sherman, December 31, 1896.
2. Greenslet, p. 26.
3. Frederick Nelson Adkins, *Fitz-Greene Halleck* (New Haven, 1930), p. 329.
4. William Winter, *Old Friends* (New York, 1909), p. 364.
5. Greenslet, p. 33.
6. *Ibid.*, p. 37.
7. *Ibid.*, p. 47.
8. Frank Luther Mott, *A History of American Magazines 1865-1885* (Cambridge, 1938), II, 454.
9. Greenslet, p. 48.
10. *Ibid.*, p. 53.
11. *Ibid.*, p. 82.
12. Paul Elmer More, "Thomas Bailey Aldrich," *Shelburne Essays, Seventh Series* (Boston, 1908), p. 152.
13. Fred Lewis Pattee, *A History of American Literature Since 1870* (New York, 1917), p. 133.
14. Letter, Howells to Aldrich, March 21, 1869. Widener Library.
15. Gilbert Donaldson, "Thomas Bailey Aldrich," *The Reader,* IX (May, 1907), 658ff.
16. Alexander Cowie, *The Rise of the American Novel* (New York, 1948), p. 580.

17. William Dean Howells, "Recent Literature," *Atlantic*, XXXII (November, 1873), 625.

18. Eunice E. Comstock, "Marjorie Daw," *Atlantic*, XXXII (November, 1873), 610.

19. Cowie, *op. cit.*, p. 585.

20. William Dean Howells, "Mr. Aldrich's Fiction," *Atlantic*, XLVI (November, 1880), 697.

21. Greenslet, p. 194.

22. All Academy data in Walter Read, "The Membership in Proposed Academies," *American Literature*, VII (May, 1935), 145-65.

23. *Works*, II, 182.

24. *Works*, II, 72.

25. H. L. Mencken, *A Book of Prefaces* (New York, 1924), p. 215.

26. Hartley Grattan, "Thomas Bailey Aldrich," *American Mercury*, X (May, 1925), 44.

27. Vernon Louis Parrington, *Main Currents in American Thought*, III (New York, 1927), 57.

28. Willard Thorp, "Defenders of Ideality," in *Literary History of the United States*, ed. Robert Spiller and Willard Thorpe (New York, 1948), p. 4.

Selected Bibliography

PRIMARY SOURCES

The Bells. A Collection of Chimes. New York: J. C. Derby, 1855.
Daisy's Necklace and What Came of It. A Literary Episode. New York: Derby and Jackson, 1857.
The Course of True Love Never Did Run Smooth. New York: Rudd and Carleton, 1858.
The Ballad of Babie Bell, and Other Poems. New York: Rudd and Carleton, 1859.
Pampinea, and Other Poems. New York: Rudd and Carleton, 1861.
Out of His Head. A Romance. New York: G. W. Carleton, 1862.
Poems. New York: G. W. Carleton, 1863.
The Poems of Thomas Bailey Aldrich. Boston: Ticknor and Fields, 1865.
The Story of a Bad Boy. Boston: Fields, Osgood and Co., 1870.
Marjorie Daw and Other People. Boston: J. R. Osgood and Co., 1873.
Cloth of Gold and Other Poems. Boston: J. R. Osgood and Co., 1874.
Prudence Palfrey. A Novel. Boston: J. R. Osgood and Co., 1874.
Miss Mehetabel's Son. Boston: J. R. Osgood and Co., 1877.
A Rivermouth Romance. Boston: J. R. Osgood and Co., 1877.
A Midnight Fantasy, and the Little Violinist. Boston: J. R. Osgood and Co., 1877.
The Queen of Sheba. Boston: J. R. Osgood and Co., 1877.
The Stillwater Tragedy. Boston: Houghton, Mifflin and Co., 1880.
Friar Jerome's Beautiful Book, and Other Poems. Boston: Houghton, Mifflin and Co., 1881.
XXXVI Lyrics and XII Sonnets. Boston: Houghton, Mifflin and Co., 1881.
From Ponkapog to Pesth. Boston: Houghton, Mifflin and Co., 1883.
Mercedes, and Later Lyrics. Boston: Houghton, Mifflin and Co., 1884.
The Poems of Thomas Bailey Aldrich. Boston and New York: Houghton, Mifflin and Co., 1885.

Wyndham Towers. Boston and New York: Houghton, Mifflin and Co., 1890.

The Sisters' Tragedy, with Other Poems, Lyrical and Dramatic. Boston and New York: Houghton, Mifflin and Co., 1891.

An Old Town by the Sea. Boston and New York: Houghton, Mifflin and Co., 1893.

Two Bites at a Cherry, with Other Tales. Boston and New York: Houghton, Mifflin and Co., 1894.

Unguarded Gates, and Other Poems. Boston and New York: Houghton, Mifflin and Co., 1894.

Later Lyrics. Boston and New York: Houghton, Mifflin and Co., 1896.

Judith and Holofernes. A Poem. Boston and New York: Houghton, Mifflin and Co., 1896.

The Poems of Thomas Bailey Aldrich. Boston and New York: Houghton, Mifflin and Co., 1897.

A Sea Turn and Other Matters. Boston and New York: Houghton, Mifflin and Co., 1902.

Ponkapog Papers. Boston and New York: Houghton, Mifflin and Co., 1904.

A Book of Songs and Sonnets Selected from the Poems of Thomas Bailey Aldrich. Boston and New York: Houghton, Mifflin and Co., 1906.

SECONDARY SOURCES

I. *Biography and Criticism*

ALDRICH, MRS. THOMAS BAILEY. *Crowding Memories.* Boston and New York: Houghton, Mifflin & Co., 1920. A supplement to Greenslet's biography, mostly an account of Aldrich's social life, his friendship with Clemens, Howells, and others.

ALLEN, GAY WILSON. *American Prosody.* New York: American Book Co., 1935. Contains an analysis of Aldrich's versification.

BICKNELL, PERCY F. "The Story of A Poet's Life," *The Dial*, XLV (October 19, 1908), 25-52. A favorable review of Greenslet's biography of Aldrich.

BISHOP, WILLIAM HENRY. "Authors at Home. T. B. Aldrich on Beacon Hill, and Round It," *The Critic*, VII (August 8, 1885), 61-63. An account of the luxurious life of Aldrich's at 59 Mt. Vernon Street, Ponkapog, and Deer Cove at Lynn, Massachusetts.

Selected Bibliography

BOYNTON, H. W. "Thomas Bailey Aldrich," *Putnam's Monthly*, II (June, 1907), 259-66. Some discerning criticism of Aldrich's poetry.

BROOKS, VAN WYCK. *Howells and His World*. New York: E. P. Dutton & Co., Inc., 1959. Recounts Howells' approval of *The Story of a Bad Boy* and its possible influence on Howells' own work.

BROWN, EDITH BAKER. "Thomas Bailey Aldrich," *The North American Review*, CLXXXIX (January, 1909), 130-35. A review of Greenslet's biography with high praise for author and subject.

CLEMENS, SAMUEL L. *The Autobiography of Mark Twain*, ed. CHARLES NEIDER. New York: Harpers, 1959. Clemens' extravagant praise of Aldrich's brilliant conversation.

COWIE, ALEXANDER. *The Rise of the American Novel*. New York: American Book Co., 1948. The best, fairest, most comprehensive treatment of Aldrich's fiction.

DEVOTO, BERNARD. *Mark Twain in Eruption*. New York: Grosset & Dunlap, 1940. A caustic account of the opening of the Aldrich museum in Portsmouth, New Hampshire.

DONALDSON, GILBERT. "Thomas Bailey Aldrich," *The Reader*, IX (May, 1907), 657-65. One of the very few and probably the last interview Aldrich ever gave.

FAWCETT, EDGAR. "Mr. Aldrich's Poetry," *Atlantic*, XXXIV (December, 1874), 671-75. An important review of *Cloth of Gold and Other Poems*.

FIELDS, ANNIE. *Letters of Sarah Orne Jewett*. Boston and New York: Houghton, Mifflin Co., 1911. Contains some letters to Aldrich.

GARLAND, HAMLIN. *Roadside Meetings*. New York: The Macmillan Co., 1930. An unfavorable view of Aldrich as editor of *Atlantic*.

GRATTAN, HARTLY. "Thomas Bailey Aldrich," *American Mercury*, X (May, 1925), 41-45. A scathing, biased evaluation of Aldrich's verse.

GREENSLET, FERRIS. *Thomas Bailey Aldrich*. Boston and New York: Houghton, Mifflin and Co., 1908. The official Aldrich biography containing many good Aldrich letters.

————. *Under the Bridge*. New York: Literary Classics, Inc., 1943. Contains letter about Aldrich from Woodberry pointing out that Aldrich was a warmer person than Greenslet's biography shows.

HOWELLS, WILLIAM DEAN. *Heroines of Fiction.* New York and London: Harper and Brothers, 1901. An appreciation of *Marjorie Daw*: "She will live though Aldrich destroyed her."

————. "Mr. Aldrich's Fiction," *Atlantic,* XLVI (November, 1880), 695-98. An important contemporary assessment of Aldrich's fiction.

————. "Recent Literature," *Atlantic,* XXXII (November, 1873), 625-26. A review of *Marjorie Daw and Other People,* with Howells rightly preferring "Marjorie Daw," "A Struggle for Life," and "A Rivermouth Romance."

————. "Recent Literature," *Atlantic,* XXXIV (August, 1874), 227-29. A friendly review of *Prudence Palfrey.*

————. "Recent Literature," *Atlantic,* XLI (January, 1878), 141. A review of *The Queen of Sheba.*

————. "Reviews and Literary Notices," *Atlantic,* XXV (January, 1879), 124. Howells reviews *The Story of a Bad Boy* as a new thing in American literature.

————. *Suburban Sketches.* Boston: J. R. Osgood and Co., 1875. Aldrich's and Howells' experience as editors in Boston.

MABIE, HAMILTON W. "An Appreciation," *Bookman,* LXXXIV (November 24, 1906), 735-38. A biographical, anecdotal sketch.

————. "An Appreciation," *Outlook,* LXXXIV (November, 1906), 735. A good biographical sketch.

MANGUM, CHARLES R. *A Critical Biography of Thomas Bailey Aldrich.* Cornell University, 1950. An unpublished dissertation.

MOODY, WILLIAM VAUGHN. "Our Two Most Honored Poets," *Atlantic,* LXXXI (January, 1898), 136. A review of the eight-volume Riverside edition of Thomas Bailey Aldrich. Moody praises Aldrich for "holding up an ideal of workmanship so sound, in a generation where the temptations to flashy devices are so many. . . ."

MORE, PAUL E. *Shelburne Essays, Seventh Series.* New York and London: G. P. Putnam's Sons, 1910. One of the best evaluations of Aldrich's poetry and a definition of *vers de société,* a genre Aldrich excelled in.

MORSE, JAMES HERBERT. "Thomas Bailey Aldrich," *The Critic,* XXXI (December, 1897), 335. An appreciative article— Aldrich's verse the best thing of its kind in America.

PAINE, ALBERT B. (ed.). *Mark Twain's Letters.* 2 vols. New York and London: Harper & Brothers, 1917. Interesting letters from Clemens to Aldrich.

Selected Bibliography

PATTEE, FRED LEWIS. *A History of American Literature since 1870*. New York: The Century Co., 1917. A judicial assessment of Aldrich's poetry.

PERRY, BLISS. *Park-Street Papers*. Boston and New York: Houghton, Mifflin Co., 1908. A critical appreciation of Aldrich's prose and poetry by an *Atlantic* editor who knew him.

————. "Two Books by Mr. Aldrich," *Atlantic*, LXXXXII (November, 1903), 711-14. A review of *Ponkapog Papers* and *A Sea Turn and Other Matters*, stating that Aldrich was a discriminating, urbane, informed, and witty talker rather than a professional literary critic.

PHELPS, ALBERT. "The Value of Aldrich's Verse," *Atlantic*, C (August, 1907), 244. An important, discerning evaluation of Aldrich's poetry.

RIDEING, WILLIAM H. "Glimpse of T. B. Aldrich," *Putnam's Monthly and Critic*, VII (January, 1910), 398-406. A portrait of Aldrich by a friend, the editor of the *North American Review*.

————. *The Boyhood of Living Authors*. New York: Thomas Y. Crowell & Co., 1887. A charming acount of Aldrich's boyhood.

SMITH, HENRY NASH and GIBSON, WILLIAM M. *Mark Twain–Howells Letters*. Cambridge: Belknap Press of Harvard University Press, 1960. Some references to Aldrich, anecdotes, etc.

SPILLER, ROBERT, and THORP, WILLARD (eds.). *Literary History of the United States*. 3 vols. New York: Macmillan, 1948. Thorp's selection, "Defenders of Ideality," Volume II, is an excellent evaluation of Aldrich's poetry. Notes relation to imagists.

STEDMAN, E. C. *Poets of America*. Boston and New York: Houghton, Mifflin Co., 1885. Favorable reference to Aldrich, but Stedman does not treat him as he does Bayard Taylor.

TAYLOR, BAYARD. *Critical Essays and Literary Notes*. New York: Putnam Co., 1880. A review written in 1877 of *Flower and Thorn*. Taylor praises Aldrich for clarity, polish and his light, airy humor.

TAYLOR, WALTER FULLER. *A History of American Letters*. New York: American Book Co., 1947. Fuller obviously accepts Grattan's opinion of Aldrich.

"Thomas Bailey Aldrich." *Columbia University Course in Literature*. Vol. XVIII. New York: Columbia University Press, 1929. A somewhat flattering assessment of Aldrich's work.

TICKNOR, CAROLINE. *Glimpses of Authors.* Boston and New York: Houghton, Mifflin Co., 1922. Mention of Aldrich's wit, manners and careful dress. An account of the opening of the Thomas Bailey Aldrich memorial museum in Portsmouth, New Hampshire.

TRAUBEL, HORACE. *With Walt Whitman in Camden, March 28– July 14, 1888.* Vol. I. Boston: Small, Maynard, 1906; *July 16–October 31, 1888.* Vol. II. New York: D. Appleton, 1908; *March 28–July 14, 1888; November 1, 1888–January 20, 1889.* Vol. III. New York: M. Kennedy, 1914. Whitman's reminiscences of Aldrich.

TUTTLE, DONALD R. *Thomas Bailey Aldrich's Editorship of the Atlantic Monthly.* Western Reserve University, 1939. An unpublished dissertation containing a detailed examination of Aldrich's editorial correspondence.

WAGENKNECHT, EDWARD. *Cavalcade of the American Novel.* New York: Henry Holt & Co., 1952. A brief but appreciative notice of Aldrich's fiction.

WEDDER, HENRY C. *American Writers of Today.* Chicago: Silver, Burdett & Co., 1899. An evaluation of Aldrich, better than usual from one who did not share his opinions.

WINTER, WILLIAM. *Old Friends: Being Literary Recollections of Other Days.* New York: Moffat, Tard and Co., 1909. An important source, good for background of Bohemia. Some early Aldrich letters included.

WOODBERRY, G. E. "Mr. Aldrich's New Volume," *Atlantic,* LXVII (March, 1891), 402-5. An intelligent review of *The Sisters' Tragedy.*

II. *Background*

AUSTIN, JAMES C. *Fields of the Atlantic Monthly.* San Marino, California: Huntington Library Press, 1953. An important study of *The Atlantic* and its famous editor and publisher.

BEATTY, RICHMOND C. *Bayard Taylor: Laureate of the Gilded Age.* Norman: University of Oklahoma Press, 1936. An important biography of one of Aldrich's closest friends. Interesting data about literary scene in nineteenth-century New York.

BEERS, HENRY A. *Nathaniel Parker Willis.* Boston and New York: Houghton, Mifflin Co., 1885. Portrait of an important nineteenth-century editor and writer who employed Aldrich and gave him essential advice on editing.

Selected Bibliography

BROOKS, VAN WYCK. *New England Indian Summer.* New York: E. P. Dutton & Co., Inc., 1940. Establishes tone for the age in which Aldrich flourished.

CARPENTER, FREDERIC I. "The Genteel Tradition: A Re-Interpretation," *New England Quarterly,* XV (September, 1942), 427-43. A brilliant distinction between "genteel" and "merely genteel."

CARY, RICHARD. *The Genteel Circle: Bayard Taylor and His New York Friends.* Ithaca: Cornell University Press, 1952. An unsympathetic view of Taylor and his friends of the genteel tradition.

CHAMBERLAIN, ALLEN. *Beacon Hill.* Boston and New York: Houghton, Mifflin, Co., 1925. Interesting local color.

CURTIS, GEORGE WILLIAM. *The Potiphar Papers.* New York: G. P. Putnam & Co., 1853. An indignant if somewhat heavy-handed satire of "contemporary society" in New York City.

FRANCIS, SUSAN M. "The 'Atlantic's' Pleasant Days in Tremont Street," *Atlantic,* C (November, 1907), 716. An interesting account of *The Atlantic* by Aldrich's editorial assistant.

HERRON, IMA HONAKER. *The Small Town in American Literature.* New York: Pageant Books, 1959. The literary context of *The Story of a Bad Boy.*

HIGGINSON, THOMAS WENTWORTH. *Cheerful Yesterdays.* Boston and New York: Houghton, Mifflin Co., 1898. The Boston world Aldrich admired.

HOWE, M. A. DEWOLFE. *Memories of A Hostess.* Boston: Atlantic Monthly Press, 1922. Useful for background and some discriminating remarks on Aldrich.

————. *The Atlantic Monthly and Its Makers.* Boston: Atlantic Monthly Press, 1919. An informative account of the making of *The Atlantic.*

HOWELLS, WILLIAM DEAN. *Literary Friends and Acquaintances.* New York and London: Harper and Bros., 1900. Contains an account of Howells' first meeting with Aldrich.

————. "Recollections of an 'Atlantic' Editorship," *Atlantic,* C (November, 1907), 605. ". . . and now Aldrich, my time-mate, my work-mate, my play-mate, is gone."

KNIGHT, S. GRANT. *James Lane Allen and the Genteel Tradition.* Chapel Hill: University of North Carolina Press, 1935. Useful for popular taste at turn of century and a defense of the genteel tradition.

MILNE, GORDON. *George William Curtis and the Genteel Tradition.*

Bloomington: University of Indiana Press, 1956. Contains a
good chapter on the Genteel Tradition.

MOTT, FRANK LUTHER. *A History of American Magazines 1865-
1885*. Cambridge: Harvard University Press, 1938. The
standard, authoritative history.

PATTEE, FRED LEWIS. *The Feminine Fifties*. New York: D. Apple-
ton-Century Co. Inc., 1940. A delightful and useful account
of the literary scene from 1850 to 1860.

PIERSON, ERNEST DeLANCEY (ed.). *Society Verse by American
Writers*. New York: Benjamin Co., 1887. A collection of light
verse, a genre in which Aldrich excelled.

STILL, BAYARD. *Mirror for Gotham: New York as seen by Con-
temporaries from Dutch Days to the Present*. New York:
New York University Press, 1956. Good for life in New York
City in the 1850's and '60's.

TAYLOR, BAYARD. *John Godfrey's Fortunes*. New York: G. P.
Putnam, 1865. An amusing satirical novel about New York's
Bohemian life.

WEEKS, EDWARD and FLINT, EMILY (eds.). *Jubilee; One Hundred
Years of The Atlantic*. Boston: Little, Brown, 1957. Of some
interest for its account of *The Atlantic* and its editors, including Aldrich.

WHITING, LILIAN. "Literary Boston," *Cosmopolitan*, X (December,
1890), 205-16. Interesting local color.

Index